THE FACT OR

LOST CIVILIZATIONS

FICTION FILES

FICTION

OTHER BOOKS IN THE FACT OR FICTION FILES SERIES

UFOs
Ghosts
Vanished!

THE FACT OR FICTION FILES

LOST CIVILIZATIONS

Dorothy and
Thomas Hoobler

WALKER AND COMPANY ✹ NEW YORK

First published in the United States of America in 1992
by Walker Publishing Company, Inc.

Published simultaneously in Canada by Thomas Allen & Son
Canada, Limited, Markham, Ontario

Library of Congress Cataloging-in-Publication Data
Hoobler, Dorothy.
Lost civilizations / Dorothy and Thomas Hoobler.
p. cm. — (The fact or fiction files)
Includes bibliographical references (p. 78) and index.
Summary: Examines such archaeological remains as Stonehenge, the
Easter Island statues, and the Minoan ruins on Crete and speculates
about the vanished civilizations that built them.
ISBN 0-8027-8152-7 (c)—ISBN 0-8027-8153-5 (r)
1. Civilization, Ancient—History—Juvenile literature.
2. Extinct cities—History—Juvenile literature. 3. Lost
continents—History—Juvenile literature.
4. Archaeology—History—
Juvenile literature. [1. Civilization, Ancient. 2. Antiquities.
3. Archaeology.] I. Hoobler, Thomas. II. Title. III. Series.
CB311.H63 1992
930—dc20 91-35015
CIP
AC

Printed in the United States of America

2 4 6 8 10 9 7 5 3 1

Our thanks to Fernando Olea of the Mexican Government Tourism Office in New York, Nicos Velonis of the Greek National Tourist Organization, Ruth Bandera of Ladeco Airlines, Tauni Graham of the Ohio Historical Society, and Sue Woodley of the British Tourist Authority. As ever, we are grateful to Amy Shields, Bebe Willoughby, and Georg Brewer at Walker and Company for their encouragement, advice, and patience.

THE FACT OR

LOST CIVILIZATIONS

FICTION FILES

FICTION

CHAPTER ONE:
THE STONEHENGE PEOPLE

W riting in the year 1136, Geoffrey of Monmouth set out to tell the history of the kings of England. He was more a storyteller than a historian, and he gave the world one of its very best stories when he wrote about King Arthur and his Court.

Geoffrey didn't invent King Arthur. Legends about Arthur had been popular in Wales, the western peninsula of the British island, for a long time before Geoffrey wrote. But he was the first to put these legends together in the shape they have today. And it was Geoffrey who wrote that Stonehenge was the work of Merlin the Magician.

MERLIN — THE BUILDER OF STONEHENGE?

As Geoffrey tells the story, King Aurelius Ambrosius, the uncle of King Arthur, had been fighting his neighbors, the Saxons. Some of Aurelius's men had been killed, and he wanted to build a monument in which to bury them.

Merlin suggested that Aurelius steal the "Giants' Ring," which was on Mount Killaraus in Ireland. Merlin said the Giants' Ring was made up of huge stones that had been brought from Africa in a long-ago time when giants lived in Ireland.

Merlin told Aurelius that "the stones are enormous and there is no one alive strong enough to move them. If they are placed in position round this site . . . they will stand for ever." Merlin added that the stones had magical properties.

Aurelius sent his brother Uther Pendragon (later to be King Arthur's father) to Ireland to get the stones. After a battle with the Irish, who wanted to keep the stones, Uther's men took possession of the Giants' Circle. However, try as they might with "hawsers and ropes and scaling-ladders," they could not move the stones.

Merlin had known all along that he would get a chance to show off his magic. Geoffrey doesn't give the details — Merlin, like all good magicians, kept his secrets. But he put the stones aboard Uther's ships and brought them home. Aurelius summoned all his people for a great celebration on the Christian feast of Whitsunday.

Even in his own time, Geoffrey of Monmouth was regarded as too creative for a historian. Later in the twelfth century, William of Newburgh, who also wrote historical chronicles, condemned Geoffrey's work. "It is quite clear," wrote William, "that everything this man wrote . . . was made up, partly by himself and partly by others, either from an inordinate love of lying, or for the sake of pleasing the Britons."

Modern historians say that if King Arthur ever did exist, he was a chief of a small group of Welsh tribes. His men didn't wear armor and ride in medieval tournaments. They wore skins and fought savage battles with bronze axes. And they probably knew nothing about Christianity, though Geoffrey has them celebrating Christian feast days.

Yet Geoffrey's stories, though we cannot accept them as history, contain tantalizing clues to the true purpose of Stonehenge, the great stone circle on Salisbury Plain in southern England.

We can see that even in the twelfth century, tradition held that the building stones of Stonehenge came from far away. We know that is true. It was a burial place for heroes—and human remains have been found in the Aubrey holes inside the ring. Furthermore, the stones of Stonehenge were believed to have some magical purpose. We will see shortly what that might have been.

The most important clue in Geoffrey's story was Stonehenge's supposed dedication on the feast of Whitsunday. Whitsunday comes seven weeks after Easter, and falls around the time of the summer solstice (June 24). That is midsummer day, when the sun reaches its highest point in the sky, the longest day of the year. Many ancient people celebrated this day and found ways to determine it accurately. Stonehenge was designed to mark that event.

ROMANS, DANES, AND DRUIDS

Between the twelfth century and today, more writers have offered theories on who built Stonehenge. Some said it was the Romans, who invaded England in the year 54 B.C. and conquered parts of it in the next century. Others claimed that it was built by the Danes, who controlled parts of England from the eighth to the eleventh centuries A.D. Today, we know that Stonehenge was raised long before either the Romans or the Danes reached Britain.

Another explanation of Stonehenge's origins is that it was built by the Druids. These were priests of the Celtic tribes who inhabited Britain when the Romans arrived. Indeed, the Druids' religion had spread into parts of modern-day

France as well. Julius Caesar mentions the Druids in his history of the wars he fought against the Gauls, the people who lived in France at that time.

Caesar wrote of the Druids: "It is said that they learn by heart a vast number of verses. . . . They consider it a crime to entrust these matters to writing. . . . They teach many things concerning the stars and their motions." As we shall see, the creators of Stonehenge might have known a great deal about the stars.

Other Roman and Greek writers also gave brief accounts of the Druids and their ceremonies. There is no doubt that Druid priests were once powerful in northern Europe and Britain. They are *not* a legend, like King Arthur and his knights. Even so, our knowledge of them is sketchy, since they seem to have had no writing of their own.

But most modern scholars dismiss the idea that the Druids could have had anything to do with Stonehenge. Accounts of the Druid religion did not appear until centuries after Stonehenge was completed. Furthermore, the Druids practiced their religion in woods and groves— not in stone temples. But we do not know how long the Druids had been in Britain. They may have continued some religious traditions that stretch back to the time of Stonehenge.

We do know that the conquering Romans tried to stamp out the Druids' religion. Could this account for the fact that many of the stones at Stonehenge have been knocked over or removed? If so, it would indicate that the Romans thought Stonehenge was a Druid center.

In the nineteenth century, a group of modern Britons revived the Druids' religion, based on the few details that are known about them—and a lot of imagination. These modern Druids hold a ceremony at Stonehenge each year at the summer solstice. Salisbury Plain turns into a festival that resembles a rock concert. People gather from all over Britain to witness the "sacred" rites of the self-appointed Druid priests and priestesses. Blue-jeaned teenagers climb to the top of the sarsen trilithons to get the best view of the ceremonies.

As the white-robed modern Druids move in a line through the crowd, the spectators chant supposed Druid hymns. Virtually none of this is based on any real knowledge of Druidism. But it is a link with the past.

When the summer solstice is over, the broken bottles and other debris left by the crowds are cleared away. Scientists once more take over Stonehenge, trying to sweep back the dust of centuries to determine what really went on here 5,000 years ago.

THE STONEHENGE BUILDERS

Before the 1940s, archaeologists thought that the Stonehenge people must have learned how to build from other European peoples. People saw a resemblance between Stonehenge and stone tombs in France and Spain. It even resembled, in a crude way, Greek temples found in Mycenae. Scientists believed that knowledge of how to raise large stones spread from the mainland to Britain.

However, in the past few decades, that theory has been discarded. Scientists discovered carbon dating, a way of determining how old certain objects are. Carbon dating is important to many of the other stories in this book, so we will explain a little about it here.

Everything that was once part of a living being—a bone, a piece of wood, even charcoal—has a small amount of radioactive carbon atoms within it. (You have some in your body.) When the animal or plant dies, this radioactive carbon begins to decrease. By testing how much is left in objects found in the Stonehenge ditches, scientists could tell how old they were. They made an amazing discovery. Stonehenge was built long before the temples in Greece or the stone tombs in France and Spain.

This meant that the Stonehenge people learned how to build on their own. Any clues to their civilization must lie somewhere in Britain.

The earliest people who may have been connected with Stonehenge are the Windmill Hill people. Windmill Hill, where their artifacts have been found, is the site of a great earthen circle, around 250 feet across. As you know, a similar circle was the first part of Stonehenge to be built.

The Windmill Hill people are also notable because they did not dig holes in the ground to bury their dead. Instead, they made mounds of earth—called barrows—in which they placed the dead. Many such barrows have been found on Salisbury Plain near (but not at) Stonehenge.

Some archaeologists think that this special kind of burial was intended to honor great chiefs or priests. This is an important clue to the Stonehenge mystery. For in order to build Stonehenge, large groups of people had to work together for a long time. Only a powerful leader could have organized and commanded such a project.

Archaeologists have found that sometime after the Windmill Hill people, another group appeared in Britain, called the Beaker folk. They are named after a distinctive kind of pottery that has been found in their living places. The Beakers are known to have built stone circles. One of these is a double circle of stones like Stonehenge II. It seems to have been built on an earlier earthen circle—again like Stonehenge II. Could the Beaker folk have built the second phase of Stonehenge?

Further evidence is found in the Beakers' graves. They contain axes made of bluestone, the special kind of stone that was used for Stonehenge II. Other bluestone objects seem to indicate that this type of stone was thought to have magical powers. This reminds us of the tales of Geoffrey of Monmouth.

As we know, however, the bluestones came from the Prescelly Mountains, not from Ireland as Geoffrey claimed. Patrick Crampton, a modern writer, thinks that the ancient Britons revered bluestone because they believed the Prescelly Mountains were the home of ancient gods. Crampton wrote of his field trip to Prescelly to obtain bluestone samples: "I, myself, a man of this scientific age, found [the region] strangely impressive in its form, setting, and utter loneliness. . . . There was something akin to magic when I cracked a stone on a remote hill in the far west of Wales, and a distinctive mottled surface appeared that was so familiar to me at distant Stonehenge."

Stonehenge II, the circle of bluestones, lasted for only about 150 years. During that time, the people who lived around Stonehenge prospered. Their skill as farmers enabled them to grow more than enough food for their own use. They used the surpluses to trade with people farther away. Gold objects in their graves must have come from Ireland, the nearest source of gold. Certain types of beads in their graves came from central Europe.

The graves in the Wessex area around Stonehenge are filled with objects that indicate the people buried there were great chieftains. In one grave, a man five feet ten inches tall (quite tall for those days) was wrapped in a shroud fastened by amber buttons. Just above his knees was the head of a hawk. With his body was a bronze knife and a wrist guard indicating he had used bow and arrow. At his feet was a beaker, and around his body was a ring of sea urchins. He lay in a stone coffin. The stone came from a quarry eighteen miles away. Richard Atkinson, the noted expert on Stonehenge, has written that in graves such as this, "the builders of Stonehenge themselves now rest from their labors."

Atkinson says, "I believe . . . that Stonehenge itself is evidence for the concentration of political power . . . in the hands of a single man, who alone could create and maintain the conditions necessary for this great undertaking. Who he was, whether native-born or foreign, we shall never know."

In that case, one name is as good as another. In the 1950s, the British government considered restoring Stonehenge to the way it looked when it was completed. The Chief Inspector of Ancient Monuments was asked how much this would cost. He said that the question should be "referred to a Mr. Merlin, who would have the costings from when it was last done."

Was there really a Merlin behind Stonehenge,

or at least Stonehenge III, the great sarsen circle that was built in less than a century? Did he plan the final, greatest form of Stonehenge and command the Wessex people to carry out the colossal labor of building it? Scientists would not use the name Merlin, but their work points to the conclusion that Geoffrey of Monmouth may not have been such a liar after all. He just had his dates wrong.

Whatever the name of the chief builder of Stonehenge, he had some great purpose in mind. Stonehenge must contain the clues that will tell us what it was used for. A religious temple? Or something far greater?

THE PURPOSE OF STONEHENGE

One ancient written record has intrigued those who have tried to solve the mystery of Stonehenge. Hecateus, a Greek who lived in the fourth century B.C., described the journey of a Greek named Aristeas (300 years earlier.) Aristeas went in search of a legendary people called the Hyperboreans.

Aristeas heard of an island "at least the size of Sicily, [which] lies opposite the land inhabited by the Celts, out in the Ocean. . . . Apollo [the Greeks' sun god] is honored above all the gods. There are men who serve as priests of Apollo. . . . There is also in the island a precinct sacred to Apollo and suitably imposing, and a notable temple decorated with many offerings, and looking like a globe."

Does this account describe Britain and Stonehenge? The date would be three or four centuries after the completion of Stonehenge, but we don't know how long it remained an active site.

Hecateus goes on to say that "the god returns to the island every nineteen years, the period when the stars complete their cycle." As we will see, a nineteen-year period has recently been thought to have great significance in Stonehenge's purpose.

The idea that Stonehenge was some kind of calendar began with William Stukeley, an eighteenth-century English scholar. He noted that the direction Stonehenge "faced"—from the open end of the inner U through the break in the earthen circle and toward the Heel Stone— was northeast. This was the direction where the sun rose on midsummer day. Thus, its builders must have wanted to mark the location of this annual event.

Midsummer sunrise would have been an important occasion for a society that depended on farming. But Stonehenge I, the earthen mound alone, could easily have served that purpose. If that was all Stonehenge was built for, people did not have to bring bluestones from the Prescelly Mountains and enormous rocks from Marlborough.

In 1846, Edward Duke, a local clergyman, discovered that Stonehenge could also be used to determine the day of the winter solstice—the shortest day of the year. Alongside the inner edge of the great earthen circle, Duke found two smaller circles. A line drawn between them pointed to the place in the sky where the sun rose in midwinter.

By the early part of the twentieth century, scientists realized that Duke's two circles originally marked the location of stones. Furthermore, there were four stones in all—called the station stones—at different parts of the earthen ring. An astronomer named Sir Norman Lockyer drew diagonal lines between these four stones. He discovered that they marked sunrises in February and November, and sunsets in May and August. Lockyer thought that these might have been important times for a Stone Age farming community. They could have marked the days for such events as planting crops, harvesting, and slaughtering animals for the winter.

Unfortunately, Lockyer also believed that Druid priests were in charge of "reading" this calendar. He thought that Druids must have built other stone circles, less elaborate than Stonehenge, throughout Britain. This was the reason why the Druids, according to Julius Caesar, were said to have special knowledge of the heavens.

Because other scientists refused to accept the idea that Druids built Stonehenge, Lockyer's work was generally ignored until 1963. In that year, Gerald Hawkins, an American astronomer, visited Stonehenge. As he wrote later, he realized that the spaces between the stones in the sarsen circle were "astonishingly narrow . . . so small that you can hardly poke your head through." Even at the center of Stonehenge, he could not look through all the gaps between the stones at the same time. "My field of observation was being tightly controlled . . . so that I couldn't avoid seeing something." What?

Hawkins went home with an exact diagram of Stonehenge and began to feed information into a computer. Suddenly, all the stones and holes at Stonehenge, the precise measurements of each one, seemed to have a purpose. The results, Hawkins said, were "astonishing." He found that different sight lines showed not only positions of the sun in summer and winter, but positions of the moon as well.

To understand the importance of this, remember that the period of time we think of as a "month" cannot be determined by watching the sun. The sun rises and sets in slightly different places over a cycle that is about one year long (actually 365¼ days). The time period of a month is much closer to the time between one full moon and the next. It was much easier for ancient people to see the changes in the moon.

Thus, the earliest forms of calendars were based on the moon's phases. But few people had ever thought that Stonehenge was such a precise calendar.

Hawkins said that the builders of Stonehenge had two purposes. The first was to make a calendar to tell the time for planting crops. The second was "to create and maintain priestly power, by enabling the priests to call out the multitude to see the spectacular risings and settings of the sun and moon."

Hawkins claimed that the fifty-six Aubrey holes, just inside the earthen circle, were used to predict the times of eclipses. That would have been a spectacular sight, and by predicting it, the priests could indeed have gained great respect and power. Hawkins found that an eclipse of the moon *always* occurred whenever the winter moon rose over the Heel Stone out on the avenue beyond Stonehenge. This would happen every 18.6 years. That seemed very close to the ancient Greek story that the sun god returns to the land of the Hyperboreans every nineteen years. Was the return of the god marked by the earth passing between the moon and the sun?

However, if the Stonehenge priests expected an eclipse every nineteen years, their calculations would be wrong after a few cycles. Hawkins believed they could correct their predictions by counting 19 + 19 + 18. The total was 56. Thus, Hawkins concluded, the 56

Aubrey holes were used as counters to measure the eclipse cycle.

Remember the Y and Z holes, the other mysterious rings dug during the third phase of Stonehenge? Using his computer, Hawkins found a purpose even for them. Scientists had puzzled over the fact that there were 30 Y holes and only 29 Z holes. Hawkins suggested that they could be used to mark "lunar months," or the time between full moons. The actual interval is 29.53 days. Over a two-month period, this comes out to around 59 days. If a counter was placed in one of the Y and Z holes each day, it would indicate how many days until the next full moon. Hawkins said the fifty-nine bluestones would have been used for this purpose, in the era of Stonehenge III. In fact, Stonehenge was a primitive type of computer.

Many archaeologists attacked Hawkins's conclusions. They could not believe that the builders of Stonehenge were clever enough to make such calculations. Just one fifty-six-year cycle of the moon's eclipses was longer than the average lifetime of a Stone Age human. Since the people of Stonehenge had no writing system, how could they keep records that would enable them to figure out the eclipse cycle? We remember Julius Caesar's description of the Druids: "They learn by heart a vast number of verses."

Another astronomer, C. A. Newham, had carried out his own calculations without knowing of Hawkins's work. He reached many of the same conclusions. Newham pointed out that the number of bluestones within the U at the center of Stonehenge is, once again, that significant number 19. Furthermore, one of the upright stones in the Sarsen Circle is only half the size of the others. Newham explains it by counting the total number of uprights as 29½ — the number of days in a lunar month.

Not everyone accepts these ideas. The controversy continues, 5,000 years after the first builders took up their antler picks and began to make a great circle in the ground around Stonehenge. After two thousand years of construction, some later people put the last of the great stones in place. Of all the structures the human race has built, only the Great Wall of China took a longer time — and it is over 1,500 miles long! The largest of the great pyramids of Egypt was built in only about thirty years. That was within the lifetime of a single person. How could Stone Age people have kept the memory of the elaborate plans of Stonehenge over a 2,000-year period? We don't know.

What we do know is that for at least as long as the time between the birth of Christ and today, Stonehenge was the center of a thriving civilization. Its people were prosperous enough to devote much of their labor to a structure whose purpose we still do not fully understand. Generation after generation must have worked on it. People gathered there for rites and festivals, and to watch the mysterious movements of the sun and moon that their priests could predict.

They left no written record of their civilization, and over the centuries its secrets were lost. But Stonehenge remains, reminding us that 5,000 years ago, a group of people decided to build something that would last forever.

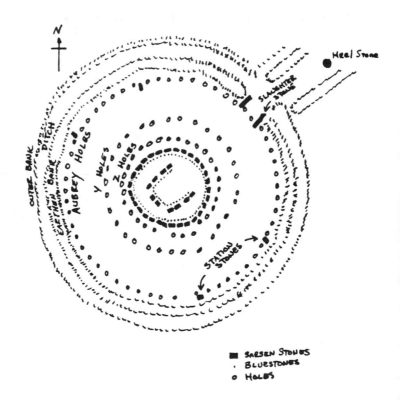

CHAPTER TWO: MYSTERIES OF ANCIENT AMERICA

THE OLMECS

Most of the awesome stone heads that the Olmecs carved more than 3,000 years ago remain on the jungle floor today. The first puzzle surrounding them is much the same as the one at Stonehenge. How could people with limited technology have constructed and moved these stones? The Olmecs had no wheeled vehicles, nor draft animals to drag the stones. At San Lorenzo, where the heads first appeared, the nearest source of stone is a mountain fifty miles away.

The task was even more difficult than the one that faced the builders of Stonehenge. For this area of Mexico is swampy; dense forests covered much of the land. La Venta, the greatest of the Olmec ceremonial centers, is on an island.

We do know that the Olmecs had rafts and dugout canoes made from light balsa wood. The only possible method of moving the stone heads, some weighing as much as thirty tons, would be to use rafts for part of the journey. They may even have gone into the Gulf of Mexico, hugging the shoreline to reach the mouth of a river, and then moving upstream.

Even so, the heads probably had to be dragged twenty-five miles from the rock quarries to a river. Once more, we have to imagine that powerful leaders—in this case, the priests of the jaguar-man cult—could command the labor of thousands of people to do the work.

The mammoth heads raise another question: Who were they supposed to represent? Some archaeologists guess that they were the images of kings. But because the heads seem to be wearing helmets, other experts suggest that they were images of those who took part in the sacred ball game. The losers in the games were executed, or sacrificed, by being beheaded.

That would also account for the fact that these gigantic sculptures were never carved with bodies. Other, smaller, examples of Olmec art typically show entire bodies. Some show physical activity such as wrestling or ball-game playing. A terra-cotta vase portrays a man resting on his elbows, with his legs twisted upward so that his feet rest on his head. A basalt pillar shaped like a man shows him staring intently upward to the heavens. No one knows for sure whether these were decorative forms of art, or if they show some of the Olmec rituals.

The two major unanswered questions about the Olmecs are: Where did they come from and why did their civilization disappear as suddenly as it began?

The first flowering of Olmec culture came in a very brief time. For some reason, scattered settlements of farmers came together to make a great earthen pyramid that would be the center of a religious cult. In doing so, they began the greatest North American culture up to that time. Their artisans created masterpieces that are far more sophisticated than any art previously known in this part of the world. It is clear that later American people, such as the Maya and the Aztecs, were influenced by the Olmecs. But why did the Olmecs lead the way?

No one really knows what provides the spark for any group of people to make the kind of leap forward that the Olmecs did. But in every place in the world where civilizations arose, fertile soil and skillful farmers played a part.

When farmers produce a surplus of food, other people can spend their time doing something besides hunting or gathering food. Artisans, priests, and scientists can make the discoveries that lead to what we call civilization. And we know that the Olmecs' agriculture was advanced enough to provide food for the priests and artists who lived in the ceremonial centers.

However, some imaginative writers still look for an outside influence that provided the spark for Olmec civilization. One of the first objects unearthed by modern scientists at La Venta was a stela, or pillar, with a carving of two people talking. One of the men had a beard; he wore a long gown and shoes with upturned toes. He looks very different from most Olmec images of themselves.

Constance Irwin, a twentieth-century writer, says that at the time this stela was carved, such shoes and dress were also worn by Phoenicians—who lived in today's Lebanon at the eastern end of the Mediterranean Sea. The Phoenicians were great seafarers, and Irwin thinks they traveled to America. That would have been a journey of over 7,000 miles.

The Olmec stone heads also bear little resemblance to the people who lived in the Americas when the Spaniards arrived. They have facial features that are more typical of Africans. Constance Irwin claims that Phoenician carvings show African slaves wearing helmets like the ones worn by the mammoth heads. The Phoenicians might have brought Africans across the Atlantic on their ships. Phoenicians also had an accurate calendar that might have provided the basis for the one that Olmec priests used.

As you will read in Chapter 3, other writers believe that sailors from the mythical continent of Atlantis might also have reached America and influenced its people. Thor Heyerdahl, as described in Chapter 5, thinks it possible that seafarers from the Middle East and Asia might have not only crossed the Atlantic but reached the Pacific Ocean as well.

All such theories imply that ancient Americans could not have developed advanced cultures on their own. But that is not true. Most scientists still think that the Olmecs developed their civilization independently.

The destruction of Olmec culture is equally mysterious. The Olmecs were not a warlike people. Olmec culture spread through trade and the appeal of the priests of its jaguar cult. Did the Olmec farmers suddenly rebel against their rulers, destroying the religious sites they had helped to build?

Or did some more aggressive people arrive? If so, why did they merely destroy the religious sites, abandoning them to the jungle? Phoenicians, for example, typically established colonies or trading posts in the places they visited. Were the Olmecs enslaved? Scientists do not have the answers to these questions.

We do know that later people continued to revere the abandoned sites of the Olmec religion. When modern explorers heard stories about them from the Indians, they searched and found the legendary lost civilization.

But the people of the jungles had never forgotten the Olmecs. Twentieth-century archaeologists report that Indians still travel down hidden paths to bring offerings to the ruined pyramids. The silent stone faces that rest on the jungle floor have kept their power to make people stand in awe and wonder. And, the old stories say, the jaguar-man still roams the mountains.

THE NAZCA LINES

The Nazca Lines in the Peruvian desert have fascinated people ever since they were discovered in the 1920s. What is the meaning of these immense pictures that can only be completely seen from the air?

One of the first scholars to investigate them was Dr. Paul Kosok of Long Island University. In 1941, Kosok declared that the Lines were "the largest astronomy book in the world." He believed that the pictures formed a zodiac, a map of the skies. It was similar to that of the ancient Greeks, who thought the constellations resembled such things as an archer, a bear, and a crab.

Because the stars' position shifts throughout the seasons, their location tells, for example, when spring is near. It would be time to plant crops. When spring comes, the rivers that start high in the Andes begin to flow strongly, providing water for the farmers in the valley below. This knowledge would be important to any ancient farmers, especially those who live in the dry areas along the Pacific coast.

Kosok's work interested Maria Reiche, a German mathematician. She devoted more than thirty years to a study of the Lines. On the ground near some of the great pictures, Reiche found small models of them. It seems certain that the builders used these to guide their work as they shifted the millions of stones needed to make the Lines.

Reiche found a picture called the Owl Man, so named because of his very large eyes. The Owl Man was a revered figure among people in the area even earlier than the Nazca civilization. The Owl Man's right arm points upward to the sky. The left arm points to the ground. Just at the spot where his right arm points, the bright star Arcturus crosses the sky in May.

Was the Owl Man supposed to be an intermediary between the world of the sky and the world of the earth?

Reiche also puzzled over the purpose of the very long straight lines that form no pictures. They stretch for miles along the plateau, and even over the hills and valleys beyond. Kosok and Reiche thought that these lines might point to the solstices and equinoxes—the points where the sun and moon reach their highest and lowest points every year. The Nazcas might have tried to make something similar to Stonehenge—a giant calendar.

Gerald Hawkins, the astronomer who claimed to find many such meanings in the arrangement of Stonehenge, began to work on the Nazca Lines in the 1960s. As part of a project cosponsored by the National Geographic Society, he fed information on the Lines into a computer. However, Hawkins could find only a few significant matchups between the Lines and the sun and moon. These could be accounted for by chance.

In the 1970s Erich von Daniken published a book titled *Chariots of the Gods.* It became a best-seller, for von Daniken claimed that people from outer space visited the earth during the distant past. As evidence he assembled all sorts of carvings and pictures that ancient people made. For example, if a carved human figure had a circle around its head, von Daniken thought it might have been a space helmet.

The Nazca Lines were exciting to von Daniken. He claimed that they were actually the tracks made by extraterrestrial aircraft—that is, flying saucers. The Nazcas deepened the lines and drew pictures to attract others to the landing place.

Maria Reiche found the landing-strip idea ridiculous. She pointed out that "once you remove the stones, the ground is quite soft. I'm afraid the spacemen would have gotten stuck."

Others tried to prove that the Nazcas themselves might have found a way to fly. How else could they have built pictures on such a large scale? Julian Knott and Jim Woodman, members of the International Explorers Society of Coral Gables, Florida, examined a piece of Nazca pottery. They found a picture of what they thought was a lighter-than-air craft, like a balloon or blimp.

Knott and Woodman set out to prove that the Nazcas could have made such a craft. They used vegetable fiber to weave ropes and a gasbag, and reeds to make a basket to carry people underneath. A group from the Explorers Society heated the air inside the bag with a fire, and the craft rose off the ground.

The passengers rose about 600 feet in the air, but then a sudden gust of wind hit the ship. It threatened to topple the balloonists out, and they swiftly landed. But after the passengers got out, the craft rose twice as high and stayed in the air for twenty minutes.

That was not the only idea that the ancient Nazcas left behind. In their graves, mummified bodies are found, wrapped in beautiful woven cloth that the dry air has preserved. Woven into one of these cloaks is a picture of masked people floating in the air. They are surrounded with ribbons. Some scientists suggest that the

Nazcas might have constructed large kites in which they flew above the earth. As far as we know, no modern adventurer has yet tried this.

Others have speculated that the Lines had a religious meaning. The Nazca, like other native Americans, believed that the earth was sacred and that spirits dwelled within creatures. Birds such as condors, hummingbirds, and seagulls were favorite subjects of the Nazca artists.

An art historian, Alan Sawyer, noted that most of the animal figures are composed of a single line that does not cross itself. (You can see this for yourself in the picture section of this book.) Sawyer speculates that the pictures are special mazes. People walking them would be participating in the life force of the animal portrayed and whatever symbolic meaning it held.

A new field called archaeoastronomy studies the ritual and worship of ancient stargazers as well as the ancients' astronomical knowledge. To the ancient Americans, astronomy was not just a science as it is today. The movements of the sun, moon, and bright planets stood for the voyages of the gods.

And the gods' wanderings had meaning for all aspects of Indian life. By following and mapping the course of the gods, one could know the fate of rulers, know when to plant, when to perform life-sustaining rituals. In order to foretell these momentous things accurately, specially trained shamans, or priests, had to accurately observe and discover the patterns of movement in the universe. Then they had to record what they saw.

In Mexico and Central America, these recordings were preserved in calendars of stone or bark books. Many are scientifically accurate. Could the Nazca Lines have a similar purpose?

The earth, too, shared in the special holy nature. It was filled with special animals, plants, spirits. Just as the gods moved across the sky, they also had their special trails on earth. Perhaps the Nazca Lines were just such mapping for the earth.

A Peruvian archaeologist, Mejia Xesspe, suggested in 1939 that the Nazca Lines might be like the sacred paths that connected Inca temples and other holy sites (700 years after the Nazcas). This idea has recently been revived by astronomer-anthropologists Anthony Aveni, Gary Urton, and Persis Clarkson. They think that the long, straight Nazca Lines were paths to guide Nazca pilgrims. When walkers reached the end, they made offerings to the gods. Other specialists have pointed out that even today in the Andes region, pilgrims walk sacred paths with offerings to sky gods.

The true purpose of the Nazca Lines may be a combination of many of these ideas. Almost certainly, they had some kind of religious purpose. Further study of them is needed, but a more urgent need is to protect them.

Today, the Nazca Lines are in danger. Though they have lasted for at least 1,500 years, their recent discovery has attracted many visitors to the area. Dune buggies and tourists tromping across the ground have left their marks on the earth around and through the lines. Aerial photographs show that the pictures are now less clear than they were thirty years ago.

Maria Reiche, who devoted much of her life to the study of the Lines, urged the Peruvian government to take action to preserve them. Today, Peru has declared the Nazca lines a national treasure and has moved to preserve this part of its ancient heritage.

THE MOUND BUILDERS

Who built the thousands of great mounds that dotted the landscape when European settlers first moved into the heartland of today's United States? The answer was all around them: the ancestors of the people who lived there, the original Americans.

However, few of the new settlers regarded the Indians with anything but contempt and fear. These people were "savages" who had to be pacified or moved out of the way. The long history of the struggle between the two peoples is well known. In the centuries after Europeans first arrived, the Indians suffered the destruction of their way of life.

The myth of the "savage" Indian could not
have endured if it were known that they had a
great culture of their own. Thus, scientists
sought to prove that the people who built the
thousands of mighty earthworks must have
been someone other than Indians. As a result, a
myth arose that a group of people called the
Mound People built the earthworks. It was believed that they had immigrated to the New
World in ancient times and then had been wiped
out by the Indians.

History holds the stories of many civilizations that vanished from the face of the earth.
Only a few of them are included in this book.
Nineteenth-century scientists had plenty of
sources to "prove" that some of those lost civilizations wound up in America.

Some said the survivors of the mythical continent of Atlantis fled westward to the New
World. Others suggested that those excellent
sailors, the Phoenicians, had come here as well
as to the Olmecs' Gulf Coast homeland.

The Norsemen of Scandinavia also had their
supporters. The governor of New York State,
DeWitt Clinton, said that the mounds in his
state had been built by Vikings. In fact, a large
pillar covered with Norse writing, or runes, was
discovered in Minnesota. This was offered as
proof that Viking sailors had explored North
America.

Others recalled certain stories told in the Bible. In the Second Book of Kings, the king of Assyria destroyed the kingdom of Israel and sent away ten of the twelve tribes of Israelites. (Only the tribes of Judah and Benjamin remained.) Ever since, legends were invented to explain what happened to the ten "lost" tribes of Israel. In 1775, James Adair, who had traded with the Indians for thirty years, wrote a book claiming that the Indians were descendants of those ancient Israelites. Ezra Stiles, the president of Yale College, was another who believed in the lost-tribe theory.

Some looked across the Pacific Ocean for the source of the Mound Builders. In 1820, Caleb Atwater, a member of the American Antiquarian Society, wrote that "Hindoos," or people from India, had crossed the Pacific "in an early age of the world." They built the mounds in imitation of the temples of their homeland. Atwater produced a three-headed pot found in Tennessee. "Does it not represent the three chief gods of India—Brahma, Vishnoo, and Siva?" he asked.

From about 1846, when the Smithsonian Institution was created, American scientists started to look seriously into Indian culture. As the techniques of archaeological detective work improved, scientists found new answers to the puzzle of the Mound Builders.

Today's scientists divide ancient America into "cultural areas." Within each of these areas, partly because of the climate and other features of the environment, the culture of various groups is similar. The Mound Builders lived in two of these cultural areas—the Northeast and the Southeast.

The Mound Builders of the Southeast appeared first—around 3,500 years ago. The earliest mounds, according to carbon dating of the artifacts they contain, were made by people in northeastern Louisiana around 1,500 B.C. The mounds had different purposes. Some were burial places, like the one Thomas Jefferson found in Virginia. Others were the sites of temples, like the one at Cahokia, Illinois.

Cahokia was probably the capital of a highly organized society that reached its height of power around A.D. 1100. Archaeologists believe that the priest-kings who lived there controlled an area about the size of the state of New York. Because of the temple's location, near a channel of the Mississippi River, it became a great trading center. Around the central mound, a log fort covered with clay was built for protection. Within this fort stood a large marketplace. Goods came to Cahokia from all over the region—furs, pottery, copper, and food.

Within the village of Cahokia, craftspeople produced goods both for use in the city and for export. Jewelers made ornaments from imported copper. They also used shells that must have been brought from the Atlantic seacoast a thousand miles away. These shells, sometimes carved with designs or made into beads, have been found among the graves of people who never saw the ocean.

Temples like the one at Cahokia have been discovered in Mississippi and Louisiana. The one at Poverty Point in Louisiana is the center of six mammoth C-shaped mounds that were built with over 1.5 million pounds of soil.

Scientists have suggested that these temple sites may have been influenced by people from Mexico, where great stone temples still existed when the Spanish arrived. Yet no artifact that can be identified as Mexican—Aztec, Mayan, Olmec—has ever been found in the culture areas of the Mound Builders.

The greatest unsolved puzzle about these southeastern temples is: Why were they abandoned? Scientists can offer only theories. One is that when women took over more of the work of farming, it freed men for warlike activities. Fighting between different groups may have caused the downfall of the whole civilization.

Cahokia itself rests on the dividing line between what scientists call the Southeast and the Northeast culture areas. It seems certain that mound building spread from the Southeast to the North very early—around 1000 B.C. Indeed, mounds have now been found from Maine to Florida, and as far west as Minnesota and Oklahoma.

Northeastern mound building reached its height along the Ohio River valley, where over 10,000 mounds have been found. Most of these were burial mounds, not temples. The sculptures, pottery, and ornaments found in these mounds show that the artists who made them were as skillful as any living in the world of that time. But we still do not understand the significance of many of their important artifacts.

The people who built the mounds along the Ohio River created what is called the Hopewell culture. Robert Silverberg, who wrote the best book on the Mound Builders, said that the Ohio Hopewell had "a flamboyant fondness for excess. . . . To envelop a corpse from head to feet in pearls, to weigh it down with many pounds of copper, to surround it with masterpieces of sculpture and pottery, and then to bury everything under tons of earth—this betokens a kind of cultural energy that numbs and awes those who follow."

Around A.D. 500 the amazing people of the Hopewell culture built the Great Serpent Mound in southeastern Ohio. This quarter-mile-long twisting snake remains today, much as it was built. Because of its unique shape, it is the most famous of the works of the Mound Builders.

The Great Serpent Mound was not a burial place; it does not contain skeletons or any burial objects. Nor does it show signs of having been used as a temple. Modern scientists believe it may have had some kind of religious function. What could it be? Why do the snake's jaws surround an egg-shaped object? Some scientists suggest that the object could be the sun, and that the Hopewells were sun worshippers.

A nineteenth-century minister claimed that the mound had been created by God, to mark the place where the serpent tempted Eve with an apple. But no one really knows.

About a hundred years ago, the owner of the land on which the Great Serpent Mound stands wanted to destroy it so the land could be used for farming. Fortunately, it was saved, but uncounted thousands of other mounds have been destroyed. Even today, bulldozers and tractors are flattening some of the mounds for housing developments, highways, or just to make room for farmers to plant their crops. Sadly, the ancient heritage of America takes second place to the needs of what we call civilization.

The complete history of the ancient Americans who came to this land at least 12,000 years ago has yet to be written. The destruction of their artifacts and holy places may make that impossible. Their civilization may forever remain among the lost secrets of the human race.

CHAPTER THREE:
ATLANTIS

In all the centuries since the ancient Greek philosopher Plato lived, educated people have read and admired his works. People have asked themselves the same questions he did, such as: What is the best kind of government? How should people treat their fellow human beings? Plato's works influenced early Christian thinkers such as St. Augustine. Though Plato lived before the time of Christ, people recognized that his thoughts on such important questions were valuable.

Thus, for centuries many people also believed Plato's story of the origins and destruction of Atlantis. Certainly, there was no way to disprove it. For no one in the nations around the

Mediterranean Sea dared to venture very far out into the Atlantic. Sailors feared that at the other end, they would sail off the end of the earth.

Educated people thought that the world might well be round. In 1492, when Columbus crossed the Atlantic and found the people he called "Indians," Europeans remembered Plato's story of Atlantis. Some suggested that the inhabitants of this New World might be descendants of the people of Atlantis.

This theory gained support when Spanish explorers discovered the Aztec empire in Mexico. The Aztecs' legends said that they had come from a place called Aztlan. The word *atl* in the Aztec language meant "water."

Other clues turned up that seemed to link Native Americans with Atlantis. As you read in Chapter 2, the Maya developed a more complicated language. It has not been fully deciphered. But a sixteenth-century Spanish priest wrote down the oral traditions of the Quiché people, a branch of the Maya. The Quiché told of their ancestors' origins in a place called Tula. In Tula, all people spoke the same language, but since leaving there, its people began to speak many languages. Tula . . . Atlantis?

Charles Berlitz, a modern-day believer in Atlantis, compiled a list of words in Native American languages that are similar to words in European or Asian languages. He compares the Mayan word *balaam* (priest) to the Hebrew word *bileam* (magician). The Quechuan word *andi,* meaning "high mountain," is the same in ancient Egyptian, where it means "high valley." Could this mean that traces of the ancient language of Atlantis are found on both sides of the Atlantic?

THE IMAGINATIVE CONGRESSMAN

Since Plato, the most influential writer about Atlantis was Ignatius Donnelly, a nineteenth-century U.S. congressman. Donnelly wrote a book, *Atlantis: The Antediluvian World,* setting forth his idea that Atlantis was the source of many of the myths and traditions of civilization. *Antediluvian* means "before the flood," and Donnelly felt that the Biblical great flood, which Noah survived by building an ark, referred to the destruction of Atlantis. Donnelly found other references to a great flood in the legends of people on both sides of the Atlantic. He claimed that all these stories drew their inspiration from the flood that sent Atlantis beneath the sea. He stated that Atlantis was the Garden of Eden, the source of civilization.

Donnelly felt that the Atlantean people settled colonies that carried on their traditions. The oldest of these colonies, he wrote, "was probably in Egypt, whose civilization was a reproduction of that of the Atlantic island."

Both the Phoenician alphabet, from which our modern one is derived, and the Mayan pic-

tographs "were derived from an Atlantis alphabet," Donnelly claimed. And "the gods and
goddesses of the ancient Greeks, the Phoenicians, the Hindus, and the Scandinavians were
simply the kings, queens, and heroes of Atlantis; and the acts attributed to them in mythology are a confused recollection of real historical
events."

Donnelly's ideas were certainly exciting. If
true, they would have overturned our usual
ideas of history, and of religion as well. But as
L. Sprague de Camp, a critic of the Atlantis
story, has pointed out, "Most of Donnelly's
statements of fact, to tell the truth, either were
wrong when he made them, or have been disproved by subsequent discoveries."

For example, it is true that many civilizations
have a myth or religious tradition that a great
flood devastated the world. However, that is
not surprising, if we consider the fact that most
of the world's ancient civilizations began in
river valleys. Rivers provided the water that was
needed for agriculture that could support large
numbers of people. As we know, all people
who live near rivers experience floods from time
to time. The stories of the disasters caused by
flooding would have been passed on to future
generations, as a warning. There is no historical
evidence that they all refer to the same flood.

Also, scientists have found no connection between Mayan picture writing and the Phoeni-

cian script. If there were, it would be much easier to decipher the Mayan inscriptions. However, none of the counterarguments have stopped believers in the Atlantis story from quoting Donnelly to "prove" their theories.

WHAT DO THE EELS REMEMBER?

Another interesting cross-Atlantic connection is found in the life cycle of the freshwater eel. For centuries, scientists knew that eels living in the rivers of Europe left their ordinary habitats to spawn, or breed. Later, it was noted that freshwater eels in America did the same thing. But no one knew where the eels' breeding grounds were.

It was not until the twentieth century that scientists found that eels from *both* sides of the Atlantic swim into the Atlantic Ocean and breed in the Sargasso Sea. The floating clots of seaweed there are ideal places for the eels to lay their eggs.

This was a startling discovery, for it made it likely that American and European eels were closely related. In addition, as you read in the Fact Files, the Sargasso Sea has often been mentioned as the possible site of Atlantis. If eels from both sides of the Atlantic originally came from that spot, it may mean that their species originated in the mysterious lost continent. Instinct causes the eels to swim "home" when the breeding cycle begins.

The lemmings of Norway display a similar kind of strange behavior. From time to time, large groups of these small rodents migrate westward toward the sea. Their behavior becomes more aggressive and frantic, and when they reach the sea, thousands jump in and swim until they drown.

Scientists admit they cannot fully account for the lemmings' strange migrations. But those who believe in Atlantis think that the lemmings too are following an ancient route to the homeland that once existed to the west. Lemmings also exist in Canada and Alaska, and they migrate, too, although not with such suicidal results.

The trouble with the lemming-homeland theory is that Norway lies far north of the place where Atlantis was said to exist. The Sargasso Sea is nearly 5,000 miles from the Norwegian coast. Unless Atlantis was so huge that it covered a much greater area than Plato described, the lemmings could not be headed for it.

A species of butterflies on the northeast coast of South America also migrates over the ocean. Flying eastward, clouds of them forge onward until they fall into the sea. It is also true that many species of butterflies are common to both Europe and America. Did they, too, spread east and west from the mysterious Atlantis?

OTHER LOST ISLANDS

The lemmings of Norway may not swim toward the Atlantis that Plato described. But other writers have described other lost islands in the Atlantic—and the Mediterranean as well—that may have some connection with Atlantis.

One old legend concerns seven Christian bishops who fled Spain when the Muslims conquered that land in the eighth century A.D. Supposedly the bishops sailed west with thousands of other Christians and settled on a large island called Antillia. They established seven cities there. This tale was still believed 750 years later when Columbus made his epic voyages. One European geographer suggested that Columbus stop at Antillia on his way to China. When European explorers found Cuba and the smaller islands near it, they dubbed them the Antilles. But no Christians lived there.

Another legendary Christian seafarer of the Middle Ages was the Irish monk Saint Brendan. Brendan was a real person, who lived in the sixth century A.D. He is best known through a manuscript written 200 years after his death. Called "The Voyage of Saint Brendan," this tale describes Brendan's attempt to find an island on which to build a monastery. Scholars think that the tale contains many reports from Irish seamen. Supposedly, Brendan found his island and returned home with news of it. For centuries, mapmakers placed St. Brendan's Island at various places in the Atlantic.

The South American country of Brazil is named for another of these mysterious islands. Mapmakers of the Middle Ages placed the Isle of Brazil southwest of Ireland. The island was rumored to be a source of red wood (brazil-wood), which European cloth makers used for making dyes. So, when a Portuguese ship landed on the east coast of South America in 1500, and the sailors found many red-wooded trees there, they called the land Brazil. But that did not stop other explorers from reporting they had found the "real" island. In 1674, a Captain Nisbet arrived in Scotland with refugees he claimed to have rescued from the magician who ruled the Isle of Brazil. Like St. Brendan's Island, the Isle of Brazil has never been found.

Although all these legendary islands were described long after Plato says Atlantis sank beneath the sea, enthusiastic supporters of Atlantis have claimed that they are remnants of the lost continent.

In fact, such tales have continued practically to the present time. Charles Berlitz, in his book on Atlantis, describes the voyage of the British ship *Jesmond* in 1882. Not long after leaving Gibraltar, Captain David Robson of the *Jesmond* noticed swarms of dead fish floating on the surface of the water. He saw smoke rising above the horizon. Sailing on, he soon discovered that the smoke was coming from mountains on a large island.

Captain Robson consulted his charts and found that they showed no land anywhere nearby. Curious, he dropped anchor and went ashore with some of his crew. According to Berlitz, they found the island had "no vegetation, no trees, no sandy beaches, bare of all life as if it had just risen from the ocean."

One of the crew spotted an unusual arrowhead in the crumbling rock of a cliff. When the crew dug into the cliff, they uncovered the remains of "massive walls." Two days of digging turned up "bronze swords, rings, mallets, carvings of heads and figures of birds and animals" and "what appeared to be a mummy enclosed in a stone case."

Robson and his men loaded these amazing objects into their ship and went on to New Orleans. There, Robson told reporters he would send the treasure trove to the British Museum. Newspapers of the time reported his discovery.

What happened to it? Disappointingly, nobody knows. Berlitz says the log of Robson's ship was destroyed in a bombing raid during World War II. The British Museum has no record of receiving any such objects. If the island was a part of Atlantis, thrust to the surface by an undersea volcano erupting, it apparently disappeared again, for no one else ever found it.

MODERN EVIDENCE FOR ATLANTIS

Artifacts like the ones Captain Robson reported would be the missing piece to the Atlantis puzzle. As you read in the Fact Files, one major reason why most scientists don't believe in Atlantis is that no physical trace of the Atlantis civilization has ever been found. If it really existed, there must be some evidence of it.

Charles Berlitz, in his book on Atlantis, cites several tantalizing discoveries that he believes may provide this hard evidence. He gives a report of Soviet deep-sea exploration off the coast of Africa in 1974. Photographs taken by Soviet researchers show walls and steps on the ocean floor. Unfortunately, after the findings were made public in 1979, the Soviet government refused to give further information about the location of the discoveries—possibly because they were looking for undersea hiding places for Soviet submarines.

Berlitz says that Spanish scuba divers found similar stone steps in the sea off the Canary Islands. Carvings on these stones "appeared to be symbols or signs that resemble 'letters' carved on rocks on land in the Canary Islands." Remember from the Fact Files that the Canaries were inhabited by people called the Guanches when Europeans first arrived. The Guanches

may have been descendants of the original Atlanteans. However, no one seems to have followed up the Canary Island discoveries.

Across the Atlantic, near the coast of the
United States, is a large shallow area called the
Bermuda Banks. Berlitz reports that airplanes
flying over this area have often spotted strange
formations under the water. "Some pilots,"
Berlitz says, "have remarked on what seemed to
be walls or roads. . . . Other pilots . . . have
suggested that some of these formations may be
the tops of buildings."

Berlitz interviewed Dr. Manson Valentine, a
scientist who had explored the sea around the
Bahamas for many years. Dr. Valentine felt that
before the end of the last ice age, much of this
area was dry land. He believed that traces of human habitation might be found there.

Dr. Valentine took photographs of the area
from a plane. He saw straight lines, squares,
and rectangles—evidence of ancient roads and
buildings. With scuba divers, he went down to
investigate. He found lines of closely fitting
stones that had been arranged to make a road.

Dr. Valentine felt he had seen roads like this
one before. He had seen the ceremonial avenue
leading to Stonehenge and another that was part
of an Olmec temple complex. Indeed, he thinks
that the people who built the undersea road also
built the Olmecs' stone heads, Stonehenge itself, and even the statues of Easter Island,

which you will read about in Chapter 5. He says the builders were "a prehistoric race that could transport and position cyclopean stones in ways that remain a mystery to us."

Atlantis itself may be the key to that mystery. If an advanced civilization rose and fell beneath the Atlantic Ocean 11,000 years ago, it may have influenced Egypt, Crete, Stonehenge, and the civilizations of the Americas as well. Or it may have been only a story invented by Plato.

If evidence of Atlantis ever appeared, it would be one of the great archaeological discoveries of all time. So far, scientists say, there is no such proof.

But scientists also thought that the Greek poet Homer's story of the Trojan War was only a myth—until Heinrich Schliemann dug up the real city of Troy in the nineteenth century. And, as you will read in the next chapter, scientists who followed Schliemann may have found another clue to the mystery of Atlantis. Somewhere, the lost civilization of Atlantis may still be waiting for a modern archaeologist to prove that Plato told the truth.

CHAPTER FOUR:
THE RIDDLE OF MINOAN CIVILIZATION

Most of what we know about the mysterious Minoans who lived on the island of Crete comes from the paintings and sculptures that they created. We might know much more about them if we could decode their writing.

As you read in the Fact Files, Sir Arthur Evans, the modern discoverer of the Minoan culture, was first drawn to Crete by clay tablets that held mysterious writing. When he unearthed the palace at Knossos, he found more examples, but he could not decipher the messages that they held.

To deepen the mystery, at least two other forms of writing have been discovered on the island. The oldest type—the one that Evans first saw—is called Linear A. A second kind, which turns up during the later period of Minoan history, is known as Linear B.

THE PHAISTOS DISK

In addition, a peculiar disk was found at Phaistos, on the other side of the island from Knossos. It held a series of symbols that were different from those on the seals of Linear A and B. This so-called Phaistos Disk is a flat clay circle about six inches in diameter. Pressed into the clay when it was wet were 241 symbols—44 different kinds in all. Many of them are clearly pictures of some object, such as a fish, a snake, a bird, a running man, or a ship. Other symbols have no clear meaning—such as circles with seven dots inside. Both sides of the disk are covered with these symbols.

The symbols are arranged in groups, with lines between each group. (Do these form sentences?) Furthermore, they are arranged in a spiral, indicating that the disk was to be "read" by turning it around—either from outside to the center, or vice versa. The clay disk was covered with a glaze and baked, which has helped it survive the ravages of 4,000 years of history. Clearly, it has some special meaning. But what?

There have been countless explanations. One scientist suggested that three symbols in one group (a snake, a bird, and the circle with seven dots) meant, "The predatory bird flies over the threshing floor in the town." Another scholar said the same three symbols read "from the sacrificial drink."

Some scientists have suggested that a Minoan seafarer may have brought the Phaistos Disk from some other civilization. But no other writing anywhere else in the world matches it.

Other experts have followed a completely different approach. They claim that the Phaistos Disk is not a form of language but an illustration. An American expert in languages, Benjamin Schwartz, theorized that the disk was a description of the holy places on Crete and a road map to guide pilgrims in reaching them.

In 1971, Leon Pomerance, an amateur code breaker, pointed out that ancient people thought the universe formed a circle. Pomerance found a circle like the Phaistos Disk on the ceiling of an Egyptian room. The Egyptian example was known to be a chart of the stars. Pomerance asked modern astronomers to reconstruct what the stars over Crete must have looked like 4,000 years ago.

When the New York Planetarium prepared a model of the ancient skies, Pomerance found a connection with the Phaistos Disk. One group of three symbols on the disk contained a snake, a bird, and a circle with seven dots. And there, in the planetarium's sky chart, were three constellations that matched these symbols—Serpens Cauda (snake), Aquila (bird), and the Pleiades (the circle with seven dots).

Many modern scientists now accept Pomerance's theory that the disk was a farmer's almanac. By comparing the stars with the symbols on the disk, Minoan farmers could tell when it was time to plant or harvest their crops.

Even if true, that tells us only what we already know—that the Minoans were an agricultural people. However, since ancient sailors also used the stars to find their way around the ocean, the disk may have been used for that purpose as well.

Why wasn't the disk written in one of the other two written scripts of Crete—Linear A and B? No one knows, and scientists continued to try to crack those codes as well. Linear B, which appeared late in Minoan history, has yielded some of its mysteries.

THE SECRET OF LINEAR B

Archaeologists also found some tablets with the Linear B script at Mycenae, in Greece. Twenty-five years before Arthur Evans dug up Knossos, Heinrich Schliemann found the site of the ancient city of Troy. Then he turned to Greece, looking for the civilization of Agamemnon, the legendary leader of the Greeks who beseiged the city of Troy. He found it at Mycenae. These ancient Mycenaeans lived in fortified palaces decorated with murals.

After Evans discovered the murals in the palace at Knossos, scientists felt that there was a connection between Crete and Mycenae. At first, they thought that the Mycenaean civilization had existed before the Minoan. After the Minoans conquered the Mycenaean civilization, they adopted parts of Mycenaean culture—including the Mycenaean writing.

But that theory was dashed after carbon dating was developed in the 1940s. Today, scientists know that the Minoan civilization was *older* than the Mycenaean.

Did this mean that Linear B spread from Crete to Mycenae? No one could tell, until Linear B was decoded.

In the 1950s, Michael Ventris, a clever British architect and amateur cryptographer, took a crack at it. He worked on Linear B, because there are many more tablets with that language than Linear A. Ventris compared Linear B with other ancient languages. Because Linear B was also found on Mycenae, he developed the theory that it was an ancient form of the Greek language.

His idea brought results, and he published a report showing that reading Linear B as Greek made sense of some of the tablets. It was a little disappointing to find that the Linear B tablets were primarily lists of objects, probably used by tradespeople. One reads, "Horse vehicle, painted red, with bodywork fitted, supplied with reins; the rail of wild fig wood with jointing of horn." It was a description of a chariot.

Unfortunately, Ventris was killed in a car accident soon after he published his first report on deciphering Linear B. But most experts agree with his findings that Mycenaean was an ancient form of the classical Greek.

Ventris's discovery meant that the Mycenaeans probably came to Crete around 1450 B.C., bringing their language with them. As you know from the Fact Files, this was the time when some kind of disaster struck the island. Was it a Mycenaean invasion? Or did some natural disaster strike down the Minoans?

THE DESTRUCTION OF MINOAN CIVILIZATION

We know that a great earthquake hit the island of Crete around 1600 B.C. But the Minoans rebuilt their palaces and restored their civilization. It survived for around 250 years. Knossos became the dominant city of the island.

Then something else happened. Not only Knossos, but all the palaces throughout the island, reverted to a more primitive way of life. Another earthquake? Probably not, for charred remains show that the palaces were destroyed by fire. The towns were abandoned.

The Minoans never recovered from this second wave of destruction. It was just before this time that the Linear B tablets—Greek—began to appear on Crete. It seems as if the Mycenaeans took over the island. What had weakened the Minoans?

Recent research on the Minoan colony of Thera produced a new theory. Thera is actually a group of islands forming a circle. A Greek archaeologist, Spyridon Marinatos, proved that a volcanic explosion of enormous force destroyed the center of Thera around 1500 B.C. The blast was so great that thirty-two square miles of Thera sank into the ocean, leaving the remnants that exist today.

Marinatos compares the destruction on Thera to the greatest volcanic explosion of modern times—on Krakatau in the Dutch East Indies in 1883. The eruption of Krakatau caused tidal waves more than 100 feet high that roared against nearby coasts, sweeping away towns and villages. Marinatos says that the explosion on Thera was four times as powerful.

Imagine, then, what might have happened on Crete, only seventy miles south of Thera. All the palaces and towns were near the coast, because the Minoans were a seafaring people. In less than half an hour, tidal waves 300 feet high struck Crete at speeds over 200 miles an hour. Clouds of volcanic ash darkened the skies for up to a year, ruining all the crops on the island. The great harbors where the Minoans' mighty ships docked were filled with silt.

The destruction must have been so great that the Minoans were easy prey for invaders. The

Mycenaeans soon arrived. The Minoans, never a warlike people, were at a grave disadvantage. The Mycenaean invaders occupied the palace at Knossos. Soon afterward, its treasures were looted and it was burned.

This account of what may have happened has one great flaw: the date of the explosion on Thera. The volcanic ash on Thera is in some places sixty-five feet deep. Underneath it are shards of pottery imported from Minoan Crete. The latest are from between 1520 and 1500 B.C.

We know that the Minoan civilization remained on Crete longer than that. The island's last artistic style was just coming into place. Minoan civilization would last slightly more than one hundred years.

Even so, the presence of Linear B tablets during this final period shows some kind of Mycenaean influence on Crete. Arthur Evans's assistant, J. D. S. Pendlebury, considered it possible that the Mycenaeans attacked and burned the palace at Knossos.

Pendlebury allowed himself to imagine that the Mycenaean attack was the source of the myth of Theseus and the Minotaur. He found evidence that a religious ceremony was actually taking place in the throne room of Knossos when the palace was burned. "It looks as if the king had been hurried there," he said, "to undergo too late some last ceremony in the hope of saving the people." Pendlebury asks: Could the king have worn the mask of a bull for this ceremony?

Theseus, as you know from the Fact Files, supposedly killed the Minotaur—half bull, half man, in the heart of the Labyrinth. Did the Mycenaeans make their way through the complicated palace—the Labyrinth—to interrupt the ceremony, and kill the king who wore the mask of a bull?

This may be too imaginative, but we know that whatever happened, the Minoan civilization had disappeared by 1350 B.C.

THERA: A CLUE TO ATLANTIS?

The explosion at Thera 3,500 years ago may also provide an explanation for another of the mysteries in this book. The disaster was so immense that it must have affected other peoples in the Mediterranean. The Egyptians would have known of it, but in their towns along the Nile River valley, they would not have felt the full force of the tidal waves.

The Egyptians, who were careful record keepers, would have preserved the story. And it may have been Thera and Crete that inspired the Egyptian story of Atlantis that Plato wrote down a thousand years after the fall of Minoan civilization.

There are some similarities between the legend of Atlantis and what really happened on Thera and Crete. As you read in Chapter 3, the people of Atlantis fought a great battle with Athens at the time when a great earthquake and flood destroyed Atlantis. Athens was only a village at the time, but Mycenae—an earlier Greek civilization—was near the height of its power. They may already have been struggling with the Minoans. And obviously, earthquakes and a tidal wave may have destroyed Crete.

Furthermore, according to the legend, Atlantis sank beneath the sea. We know that most of Thera, the Minoans' colony, actually did.

According to the legend, Atlantis had several kings—just as Crete had several palace-cities, probably with a ruler in each. When the kings of Atlantis met, Plato says they captured and sacrificed a bull, and a bull was the sacred animal of the Minoans.

On the other hand, Plato very clearly says that Atlantis was beyond "the Pillars of Hercules." These marked the entrance to the Mediterranean Sea, and so the island of Atlantis must have been in the Atlantic Ocean. Furthermore, Plato said Atlantis sank beneath the waves 9,000 years earlier. The destruction of Crete occurred only 1,000 years before Plato wrote. But Plato—or the ancient Egyptians who supposedly first told the story of Atlantis—could merely have exaggerated the time.

We do know that both the people of Atlantis and the Minoans were great seafarers. How far could they have traveled? As far as America?

Read the Fiction Files of Chapter 5, and you will see that at least one modern scientist believes that ancient people of the Mediterranean could have reached America. Someday, if the tablets with the Linear A language are ever decoded, we may learn just how great the lost civilization of the Minoans really was.

CHAPTER FIVE:
EASTER ISLAND: THE
WALKING STATUES

S cientists refused to believe the Easter Islanders' legend that the huge stone statues *(moai)* walked to their platforms *(ahu)* near the beach. Nor did scientists accept the islanders' tradition that their earliest ancestors came from the east. That could only mean they came from South America, 2,000 miles away. How could the crude reed boats that the islanders used have traveled that distance?

Scientists insisted that the islanders must be descended from some of the people who live on the Pacific islands to the west of Easter Island. These islands were also far away, but many were closer than South America. Furthermore, Captain Cook, in his eighteenth-century voyages through the Pacific, found that the Polynesians and other Pacific people sailed to and from widely spaced islands, using only the stars as a guide. Scientists now believe that over centuries the Polynesians came from Southeast Asia and gradually populated the islands of the Pacific. It seemed logical to think that in some distant time, the Polynesians arrived at Easter Island as well.

As you read in the Fact Files, certain important details of Easter Island's culture did not fit this theory. Most obvious of all was the fact that no Polynesians had built statues like the ones on Easter Island. Was this a cultural practice that developed here, and here alone?

THE TABLETS SPEAK

In addition, the strange wooden tablets covered with pictographic symbols were also unique to Easter Island. No Polynesians had a written form of language. It seemed very strange that the small population of this island had, by themselves, developed a sophisticated form of writing.

More of these tablets continued to turn up. The islanders apparently hid them in the caves beneath the island's rocky surface. In 1886 William J. Thomson, an American, found a very old man on the island who claimed he could read these *rongo-rongo* tablets. The islander, Ure Vaeiko, said he had been taught the secret before the great Peruvian slave raid of 1862 carried off the last king of the island. But Ure Vaeiko refused to read them now, because he had become a Christian and the priests had forbidden him to read these "heathen" words.

Finally, Thomson showed Vaeiko photographs of five of the tablets that had been sent to the Catholic bishop of Tahiti. Thomson said that the bishop would like to know what was written on them. Vaeiko studied the photographs and nodded. He recognized them, and began to read.

Scientists who had examined examples of the Easter Island writing thought it must be a form of boustrophedon [boo-struh-FED-on]. This long word means, "the way an ox turns in plowing." Each line of characters did not run left to right, as in our writing. Instead, at the end of one line, the next line begins right underneath, and upside down. So a person reading it has to turn the tablet, or page, each time he comes to the end of a line. (This is supposed to resemble the way a farmer using an ox-drawn plow moves up and down the rows of a field.)

And that was just the way Vaeiko read the tablet—by turning it continually as he made his way through it. Thomson was excited, and began to write down in English everything that Vaeiko read.

However, Thomson soon noticed that Vaeiko did not seem to be reading each of the pictographic "words." Thomson distracted Vaeiko, and substituted another photograph for the one he had been reading. When Vaeiko began to read again, he started the same story at the point he had left off. Thomson pointed to individual symbols and asked what they meant. Vaeiko admitted he did not know, but said that the story was the right one for this tablet. As proof, he brought another old man who knew the writing. This man read the same story that Vaeiko did.

Thomson concluded that they recognized enough of the tablets to know what story it held. Then, through memory, they retold that particular story. They knew they were supposed to make the motions of turning the tablet when reading.

This did not help decipher the writing itself. But the stories were accepted as genuine parts of the islanders' tradition.

WHERE DID THE LONG-EARS COME FROM?

Thomson heard once more that Hotu Matua, a great king, had left his country in the east and come to Easter Island. And, like the other scientists, Thomson did not believe it. He wrote, "It is difficult to account for the statement, so frequently repeated . . . that Hotu Matua came from the east . . . because the chart shows no islands in that direction."

Thomson did not consider it possible that

Hotu Matua could have come from South America. That was too far. Thomson admitted that the island might have been populated at different times by two different peoples, but thought that both had come from Pacific islands to the west.

The first person to find a link between Easter Island and South America was the travel-book writer J. Macmillan Brown. He came to Easter Island in 1923. Before that time, he had examined the Inca ruins in South America, which also contain large stone statues and walls. Though the style of these sculptures is different from the stone statues on Easter Island, Brown thought they were part of the same stone-carving tradition. When the long-ears arrived in Easter Island, Brown said, they brought this custom with them.

However, Brown had an entirely new explanation of how the stone carvers of America had found their way to Easter Island. Brown thought that a great land mass (sort of a Pacific Atlantis) had once connected Easter Island to the American mainland. Like Atlantis, it too had sunk beneath the sea, leaving Easter Island as its only remnant. Brown's absurd theory of a lost continent caused other scientists to disregard all his other observations linking Easter Island with the mainland.

Eleven years later, in 1934, another scientific expedition visited the island. Alfred Métraux, a

French anthropologist, was a student of languages. He discovered that the islanders' word for the red cylinders that stood on the heads of the statues was *pukao*. This did not mean "hat" but "topknot"—the hairstyle that many islanders wore by tying their hair up with a band. Thus, the red stones signified red hair.

As you know from the Fact Files, some previous visitors noted that many of the "white-skinned" islanders had reddish hair. This confirmed the idea that the statues were meant to depict real people, not mythical gods. And it also indicated that the very first people, the "long-ears," were red-haired and white-skinned. Who could they have been? Where did they come from?

Métraux insisted that the islanders must be Polynesians. Other people of the Pacific islands, such as the Melanesians, were quite dark-skinned. One could not call the Polynesians white, but they were the lightest of the Pacific peoples.

HEYERDAHL—THE DETECTIVE OF EASTER ISLAND

More than twenty years later, that was still the commonly accepted scientific belief. In 1955, Thor Heyerdahl, the great Norwegian adventurer and anthropologist, brought a team of scientists to Easter Island. What he found made scientists reconsider their ideas. At last, someone paid close attention to what the islanders said about themselves.

Heyerdahl was already famous for overturning a long-held scientific belief. Scientists believed that the Polynesians had populated the Pacific islands by moving eastward from Asia. Thus, there could have been no connection between the cultures of the Americas and the Polynesians. But in 1947, Heyerdahl had built a balsa log raft like the ones ancient Americans used. With five companions, he sailed westward from Peru on this raft, named *Kon-Tiki,* and reached some of the Polynesian islands. He showed that it was possible for the ancient Americans to have contributed to the Polynesian culture.

Now, eight years later, Heyerdahl was ready to tackle the mystery of the Easter Island statues. He started with the heads that stood in the earth at the base of the volcano where they were carved. Scientists had wondered why these images were only heads, while the statues that had been set up on the beach included bodies and arms.

Heyerdahl recruited a group of islanders and dug at the base of one of the heads. He found that the body was there, just as it was on all the other statues. But centuries of rain had washed silt down the hill and covered the bodies. In addition, he discovered that some of the statues farther up the hill had rounded backs. These had been used to slide the statues down the side of the mountain.

At the bottom of the mountain, the backs were smoothed off and carved with various symbols. The carvings showed two circles above three curved lines, and below that a symbol that looked like an M. Heyerdahl interpreted these as follows: the two circles were the sun and moon; the curved lines were a rainbow; the M was rainfall.

On one statue, Heyerdahl's expedition found the carving of a ship on its front. The ship had three masts with large rectangular sails. Heyerdahl thought the curved hull of the ship, rising to a point at either end, resembled the reed ships of ancient Americans. Other scientists claim that the masts and sails mark it as a European ship.

When Heyerdahl uncovered the base of one of the statues near the beach, he found a carving of a similar ship. He believed it was very old. Using the carbon-dating method described in Chapter 1 of the Fiction Files, Heyerdahl found that material in the rubble around the base was at least 1,000 years old. The carving must have been covered up long before any European ships had arrived on the island.

Heyerdahl believed strongly in trying to re-create the actions of ancient people. Years earlier, when he had told a museum director that the ancient Americans could have reached Polynesia by boat, the director said, "You try to go from South America to Polynesia on a balsa raft." And Heyerdahl did. Now, to prove that the islanders could have carved and raised the statues, he asked some of them to do it again.

The islanders thought about it. One night, Heyerdahl and the people in his camp were awakened by the sounds of singing villagers. They began to reenact an ancient ceremony that was held when a statue was to be built. No outsiders had ever seen this ritual before. But through oral tradition, the islanders had preserved the knowledge of it.

The next day, some of them took up the stone hand axes that still lay inside the volcano's cone. They sharpened the tools by pounding them against each other. And then, as a photographer recorded the work, they started to carve a new statue. They sprayed water on the rock to soften it, and the ancient image began to emerge from the rock.

Heyerdahl had proved that the knowledge of the statue builders still existed. However, he did not have the time to wait for a full new statue to be carved. Furthermore, he had not solved the problem of getting it from the volcano to the beach.

So he decided to raise one of the statues already at the beach. As you have read, all of these now lay toppled from the stone bases where they had once stood. Many had been washed into the sea and lost, but hundreds still remained. Heyerdahl picked one near his camp and recruited twelve villagers to do the job. Again, an impressive ceremony preceded the work. Then, using thin poles obtained on the island, the villagers slowly lifted the statue, which was lying on its face. "By prying up first one side and then the other," Heyerdahl wrote, "they put progressively larger stones underneath it." Finally, "the *moai* tilted on end of its own weight and stood gazing out over our camp with deep empty eye sockets." It had taken only eighteen days to do the job.

Heyerdahl went back to one of the statues near the volcano. With the help of 180 islanders, he put the statue on a crude wooden sledge and dragged it for a short distance. But the old people of the island shook their heads. That was the wrong way, they insisted. The statues were not dragged to the beach. They walked.

"But Leonardo," Heyerdahl said to one of the men, "how could they walk when they had only heads and bodies and no legs?"

"They wriggled along like this," Leonardo said, as he placed his legs together and moved his body from side to side.

Heyerdahl did not understand the meaning of that remark until 1987, when he returned to the island on another expedition. You will read about that below. For now, let's stay with Heyerdahl's 1955–56 expedition, for it yielded more important discoveries.

Heyerdahl was curious about the large holes on the rim of the volcano. The islanders insisted that poles had once been placed in these, and ropes tied to the poles to hold the statues as they were lowered into the valley below. But from the time the first Europeans arrived, no large trees to make such poles were ever seen on the island.

Heyerdahl drilled into the earth, taking soil samples from as deep as twenty-five feet beneath the surface. When scientists analyzed them later in a laboratory, they discovered pollen that proved many trees once grew on the island. One of them was native to South America. Later, Heyerdahl visited the mainland, and found trees with trunks large enough to have filled the holes at the top of the volcano.

The islanders trusted Heyerdahl enough to show him the place where the long-ears had dug the defense ditch, which became their funeral pyre. When Heyerdahl dug there, he found charcoal and ashes not far below the surface. Carbon dating showed that the date of the fire was A.D. 1676, but the date has a margin for error of plus or minus 100 years. Thus, it was possible that the great battle between long-ears and short-ears could indeed have taken place around the time when Captain Cook visited the island. Proof that yet another "myth" was true.

By now, the islanders trusted Heyerdahl enough to reveal one of their greatest secrets— one that no outsider had ever seen. They allowed him to visit some of the caves under the island. Some caves were easy to reach; they were hidden by sand or rocks in the grassy fields. Others were narrow passages in the sides of the cliffs that faced the sea. Heyerdahl had to be lowered by rope, with the sea crashing on rocks hundreds of feet below, to reach them.

He wrote:

Nothing can equal the sensation of crawling by flashlight through tunnels so narrow I had to turn my head sideways, feeling as though thousands of tons of rock were pressing on my back and chest as I forced my way through the narrow passages. And then to sit up inside a vaulted room surrounded by barbaric, bizarre, and grotesque sculptures of demons, beasts, skulls, monsters, hands, feet, and boat models carved in lava. . . . A few of these pagan hideouts were tidy and showed every sign of still being held in veneration.

Despite all the efforts of outsiders to destroy them, the islanders had preserved this part of their ancient culture. They allowed Heyerdahl to take some of the stone sculptures to his museum in Norway. Later, he published pictures of many of them in a book, *The Art of Easter Island.*

Heyerdahl believes these sculptures show a link between Easter Island and a mysterious group of people who lived on the Peruvian coast of South America before the Inca civilization arose there. He says that these pre-Incan people were white-skinned. When the Spanish reached the Inca empire in 1532, the Incas mistook them for these earlier explorers, and called them *Vira-cochas* (foam of the sea).

Inca myths said that these mysterious white people had sailed away into the Pacific. Heyerdahl believes they were the first settlers of Easter Island—the "long-ears." Hundreds of years after that, Polynesians (the "short-ears") arrived there. According to Heyerdahl, strains of both these people are still present among the Easter Islanders today.

But this theory raised another question: Where did the white-skinned people come from *before* they arrived in Peru? Red-haired and bearded, they did not resemble any of the other inhabitants of North or South America.

Heyerdahl had a startling answer to that question, and devoted much of the next thirty years to proving it. He thought that the ships with sails shown in Easter Island's art resembled "those of Egypt, Mesopotamia, and the Indus Valley"—halfway around the world.

Most scientists regard this as a fantasy, for as

Heyerdahl admits, those civilizations were separated from Easter Island "by the world's three largest oceans." But he saw the oceans as a link that ancient seafarers could cross.

Heyerdahl says that seafarers in the prehistoric Indus Valley city of Lothal are the oldest known people to lengthen their earlobes by placing plugs in them. Buddha himself, the Indian nobleman who founded one of the world's great religions, is usually depicted with these long earlobes. Another scientist claimed that the *rongo-rongo* writing tablets of Easter Island resembled a written language from ancient India.

Heyerdahl once more tried to prove his theory by practical application. He built a boat from papyrus reeds, like the ones ancient Egyptians had used. On this ship, *Ra II*, he and a crew sailed across the Atlantic Ocean in 1970.

That was not the last of Heyerdahl's adventures. Eight years later, he built another reed boat, like those the Sumerians of Mesopotamia used four thousand years ago. Sailing from the Tigris River, he went down the Persian Gulf into the Indian Ocean. He traveled to the Indian subcontinent and then went west to the coast of Africa.

In these heroic ventures, Heyerdahl proved at least the possibility of a link between ancient civilizations of India, the Middle East, and the Americas. But most scientists remain skeptical.

THE STATUES WALK AGAIN

Heyerdahl found another clue, which turned out to be a prediction. He had often wondered why the Easter Island statues had only blank eye sockets in place of eyes. Their other facial features were realistically carved—why not the eyes?

Studying stone images made in the Middle East from Mesopotamia to the Indus Valley, he realized that many of them had inlaid eyes, made of stones of contrasting colors. So did massive stone statues in Mexico and Peru. Was it possible that Easter Island's statues also had such eyes when they were first made?

On his 1955 expedition to Easter Island, Heyerdahl had befriended a young islander named Sergio Rapu. Rapu was eager to learn, and one of the other scientists brought him to the United States, where he studied to become an archaeologist. Later the Chilean government appointed Rapu to be the first native governor of the island. And then, in 1977, Rapu announced that he had found an inlaid eye that fit one of the great statues.

Heyerdahl returned to examine the find that proved his guess. Easter Island had changed much since his departure. An airport and hotels had been built, and the islanders had prospered. Under Rapu's guidance, some of the stone statues had been raised, and their crowns of red

"hair" restored. He and other young archaeologists had been digging in the area near one of
the stone bases when the eye was found. (Since
then, more eyes have been found and placed in
the statues, just as they originally were.)

In 1986, Heyerdahl led another scientific expedition to continue the work he had begun
thirty years before. He received a letter from an
engineer in Czechoslovakia. This man, Pavel
Pavel, had read Heyerdahl's earlier book about
the island. Pavel claimed that he knew how to
make the statues "walk." Heyerdahl brought
him to the island and obtained the permission
of the government to experiment on a statue.
They picked a medium-sized one that stood in
a field.

The old man named Leonardo, who had long
before argued with Heyerdahl that the statues
could walk, was still alive. He remembered the
ancient ritual for the walking-statue time, and
he and his sister sang as he strummed a stringed
instrument he had made.

Pavel Pavel tied two long ropes to the statue's
head, and two others to its base. Communica-
tion was hindered by the fact that Pavel spoke
only Czech, which no one else understood. But
by gestures and shouts, he made clear his plan.

Four groups of men took hold of each rope.
The group holding the rope on one side of the
head pulled until the base on the opposite side
rose slightly off the ground. Immediately, the

men holding the rope on that side of the base pulled—and the base moved forward.

Then, as the statue settled into place, the men holding the rope on the opposite side of the head pulled. Again, the opposite side of the base rose up, and those holding that rope jerked it forward. As the men got the idea, their timing improved, and the statue began to move across the field—just as Leonardo had once shown Heyerdahl, shuffling along with his feet clamped together.

Heyerdahl wrote:

We all felt a chill down our backs, when we saw the sight that must have been so familiar to the early ancestors of the people around us. A stone colossus of an estimated ten tons "walking" like a dog on a leash. . . . We could all read from Leonardo's face that he had known the truth the whole time: it was the song he and Elodia had sung that had made the *moai* move.

The work at Easter Island goes on today, for there is still much to discover. Heyerdahl's idea that seafarers from the other side of the world eventually made their way to this isolated spot remains unproven—to most scientists. Yet it is no more fantastic than the islanders' legends once seemed to earlier explorers. Finding the origins of that lost civilization that came to Easter Island, made these awesome statues, and caused them to "walk" could be one of the great discoveries that someone reading this book may one day make.

BIBLIOGRAPHY

Stonehenge

Atkinson, R. J. C. *Stonehenge*. New York: Penguin Books, 1979.

Castleden, Rodney. *The Stonehenge People*. London: Routledge and Kegan Paul, 1987.

Chippindale, Christopher. *Stonehenge Complete*. Ithaca, N.Y.: Cornell University Press, 1983.

Crampton, Patrick. *Stonehenge of the Kings*. London: John Baker Publishers, 1967.

Hawkins, Gerald S., and White, John B. *Stonehenge Decoded*. New York: Dell, 1965.

Piggott, Stuart. *The Druids*. New York: Thames & Hudson, 1985.

Wernick, Robert, and the editors of Time-Life Books. *The Monument Builders*. New York: Time-Life Books, 1973.

Ancient Americans

Carlson, John B. "America's Ancient Skywatchers." *National Geographic*, March 1990: 76.

Casson, Lionel, et al. *Mysteries of the Past*. New York: American Heritage Publishing Co., 1977.

Editors of Reader's Digest. *The World's Last Mysteries*. Pleasantville, NY: Reader's Digest Association, Inc., 1978.

Editors of Time-Life Books. *Barbarian Tides.* Alexandria, VA: Time-Life Books, 1987.

Helms, Mary W. *Middle America: A Culture History.* Lanham, Md.: University Press of America, 1982.

Kopper, Philip. *The Smithsonian Book of North American Indians.* Washington, D.C.: Smithsonian Books, 1986.

Krupp, Edwin C. *Echoes of the Ancient Skies: The Astronomy of Lost Civilizations.* New York: Harper & Row, 1983.

McIntyre, Loren. "Mystery of the Ancient Nazca Lines." *National Geographic,* May 1975: 716.

Silverberg, Robert. *The Mound Builders.* New York: Ballantine Books, 1974.

Stuart, George E. "Who Were the Mound Builders?" *National Geographic,* December 1972: 783.

Tompkins, Peter. *Mysteries of the Mexican Pyramids.* New York: Harper & Row, 1976.

Atlantis

Berlitz, Charles. *Atlantis: The Eighth Continent.* New York: G. P. Putnam's, 1984.

de Camp, L. Sprague. *Lost Continents.* New York: Dover, 1970.

Cazeau, Charles J., and Scott, Stuart D., Jr. *Exploring the Unknown: Great Mysteries Reexamined.* New York: Plenum Press, 1980.

The Minoans

Casson, Lionel, et al. *Mysteries of the Past.* New York: American Heritage Publishing Co., 1977.

Cottrell, Leonard. *The Horizon Book of Lost Worlds.* New York: American Heritage Publishing Co., 1962.

Edey, Maitland A. *Lost World of the Aegean.* New York: Time-Life Books, 1975.

Editors of Time-Life Books. *The Age of God-Kings.* Alexandria, VA: Time-Life Books, 1987.

Judge, Joseph. "Minoans and Mycenaeans, Sea Kings of the Aegean." *National Geographic,* February 1978: 142.

Marinatos, Spyridon. "Thera: Key to the Riddle of Minos." *National Geographic,* May 1972: 702.

Easter Island

Heyerdahl, Thor. *Aku-Aku.* New York: Rand-McNally, 1958.

———.*Easter Island: The Mystery Solved.* New York: Random House, 1989.

———."Sails in the Wake of Sumerian Voyagers." *National Geographic,* December 1978: 806.

Beaglehole, J. C., ed. *The Journals of Captain James Cook,* Vol. 2. Cambridge: Cambridge University Press, 1969.

FICTION INDEX

Adair, James, 32
America, 19–36
Antillia, 43
archeoastronomy, 28
Aristeas, 11–12
Arthur, King, 1, 2, 3, 5
Art of Easter Island, The (Heyerdahl), 72
astronomy, 28
Athens, 58
Atkinson, Richard, 10
Atlantis, 23, 31, 37–48
   lost islands related to, 43–46
   modern evidence for, 46–48
   Plato and, 37–38, 39, 42, 44, 48, 57, 58
   Thera and, 57–58
Atlantis: The Antediluvian World (Donnelly), 39
Atwater, Caleb, 32
Aubrey holes, 3–4, 15–16
Aurelius Ambrosius, King, 2–3
Aveni, Anthony, 29
Aztecs, 21, 38

Beakers, 8–9
Berlitz, Charles, 38–39, 44–45, 46, 47
Bermuda Banks, 47
Bible, 31–32
boustrophedon, 62
Brazil, 44
Brendan, Saint, 43–44
Brown, J. Macmillan, 64
Buddha, 73
butterflies, 42

Caesar, Julius, 5, 13, 16
Cahokia, Ill., 33–34
calendars, 12–17, 26, 29
Canary Islands, 46–47
carbon dating, 7, 33, 53, 67, 70
Chariots of the Gods (von Daniken), 26
Clarkson, Persis, 29
Clinton, DeWitt, 31
Columbus, Christopher, 38, 43

Cook, James, 60–61, 70
Crampton, Patrick, 9
Crete, 48, 49, 51, 53, 54, 55, 57–58

Danes, 4
de Camp, L. Sprague, 40
Donnelly, Ignatius, 39–41
Druids, 4–6, 13–14, 16
Duke, Edward, 13

Easter Island statues, 47, 60–77
   red "hair" of, 65, 74–75
   "walking" of, 60, 69, 74–77
eclipses, 15
eels, 41
Egypt, Egyptians, 17, 39, 48, 51, 57, 58, 72, 73
equinoxes, 25–26
Evans, Arthur, 49, 52–53, 56
extraterrestrials, 26–27

flying saucers, 26–27

Geoffrey of Monmouth, 1–4, 9, 11
Great Serpent Mound, 35–36
Great Wall of China, 17
Guanches, 46–47

Hawkins, Gerald, 14, 15–16, 17, 26
Hecateus, 11–12
Heyerdahl, Thor, 23, 65–77
Homer, 48
Hopewell culture, 35, 36

Incas, 29, 64, 72
India, 32, 73
Irwin, Constance, 22
Isle of Brazil, 44
Israelites, 32

jaguar-man cult, 20, 23, 24
Jefferson, Thomas, 33

Knossos, 49, 50, 52, 53, 54, 56
Knott, Julian, 27
Kosok, Paul, 24, 25
Krakatau, 55

Labyrinth, 57
La Venta, 20, 22
lemmings, 42, 43
Leonardo, 69, 75, 76
Linear A, 50, 52, 59
Linear B, 50, 52–54, 56
Lockyer, Norman, 13–14
Lothal, 73

Marinatos, Spyridon, 55
Marlborough, 12
Matua, Hotu, 63–64
Mayans, 21, 38, 39–40, 40–41
Merlin, 1, 2–4, 10–11
Métraux, Alfred, 64–65
Minoan civilization, 49–59
  destruction of, 54–57
  writing of, 49–54
Minotaur, 56, 57
moon, 14–15
Mound Builders, 30–36
Mycenae, Mycenaeans, 52, 53–55, 56, 57, 58

Native Americans (Indians), 30–31, 32, 38–39
Nazca lines, 24–30
Newham, C. A., 16–17
Nisbet, Captain, 44
Norsemen, 31
Norway, 42, 43

Ohio River valley, 35
Olmecs, 19–24, 47

Pavel, Pavel, 75
Pendlebury, J. D. S., 56–57
Pendragon, Uther, 2
Phaistos Disk, 50–52
Phoenicians, 22–23, 31, 39–40, 40–41
Plato, 37–38, 39, 42, 44, 48, 57, 58
Polynesians, 61, 65, 66, 67–68, 72
Pomerance, Leon, 51–52
Poverty Point, 34
Prescelly Mountains, 9, 12
pyramids, Egyptian, 17

Quiché people, 38

Rapu, Sergio, 74–75
Reiche, Maria, 25, 26–27, 30
Robson, David, 44–45, 46
Romans, 4, 5–6

Salisbury Plain, 8
Sargasso Sea, 41, 42
Sawyer, Alan, 28
Schliemann, Heinrich, 48, 52
Schwartz, Benjamin, 51
Silverberg, Robert, 35
solstices, 25–26
South America, 64
Stiles, Ezra, 32
stone heads, Olmec, 19–20
Stonehenge, 1–18, 19, 26, 47, 48
  bluestones of, 8–9, 12, 16, 17
  purpose of, 3–4, 11–18
  sarsen stones of, 11, 14, 17
Stukeley, William, 12
summer solstice, 4, 6
sun, 36
  Stonehenge and, 4, 11, 12, 13, 14, 15

Thera, 55–56, 57–58
Theseus, 56, 57
Thomson, William J., 61–64
Trojan War, 48
Troy, 48, 52

Urton, Gary, 29

Vaeiko, Ure, 61–63
Valentine, Manson, 47–48
Ventris, Michael, 53–54
Vikings, 31
von Daniken, Erich, 26

William of Newburgh, 3
Windmill Hill, 7–8
winter solstice, 13
Woodman, Jim, 27

Xesspe, Mejia, 29

LOST CIVILIZATIONS

THE FACT OR FICTION FILES

FACT

OTHER BOOKS IN THE FACT OR FICTION FILES SERIES

UFOs
Ghosts
Vanished!

THE FACT OR FICTION FILES
LOST CIVILIZATIONS

Dorothy and
Thomas Hoobler

WALKER AND COMPANY ✸ NEW YORK

First published in the United States of America in 1992
by Walker Publishing Company, Inc.

Published simultaneously in Canada by Thomas Allen & Son
Canada, Limited, Markham, Ontario

Library of Congress Cataloging-in-Publication Data
Hoobler, Dorothy.
Lost civilizations / Dorothy and Thomas Hoobler.
p. cm. — (The fact or fiction files)
Includes bibliographical references (p. 78) and index.
Summary: Examines such archaeological remains as Stonehenge, the
Easter Island statues, and the Minoan ruins on Crete and speculates
about the vanished civilizations that built them.
ISBN 0-8027-8152-7 (c)—ISBN 0-8027-8153-5 (r)
1. Civilization, Ancient—History—Juvenile literature.
2. Extinct cities—History—Juvenile literature. 3. Lost
continents—History—Juvenile literature.
4. Archaeology—History—
Juvenile literature. [1. Civilization, Ancient. 2. Antiquities.
3. Archaeology.] I. Hoobler, Thomas. II. Title. III. Series.
CB311.H63   1992
930—dc20   91-35015
CIP
AC

Printed in the United States of America

2   4   6   8   10   9   7   5   3   1

Our thanks to Fernando Olea of the Mexican Government Tourism Office in New York, Nicos Velonis of the Greek National Tourist Organization, Ruth Bandera of Ladeco Airlines, Tauni Graham of the Ohio Historical Society, and Sue Woodley of the British Tourist Authority. As ever, we are grateful to Amy Shields, Bebe Willoughby, and Georg Brewer at Walker and Company for their encouragement, advice, and patience.

LOST CIVILIZATIONS

THE FACT OR FICTION FILES

FACT

CHAPTER ONE:
THE STONEHENGE PEOPLE

Every summer, on the shortest night of the year, crowds of people gather at a great circle of stones in southwest England. The moon throws eerie shadows across the huge, broken stones, and it is not hard to imagine that ancient spirits have also returned. For Stonehenge — which is what people call this place now — is older than the memory of humankind. And people have kept the midsummer-night vigil thousands of times before.

As morning nears, the sky in the northeast begins to lighten. The crowd hushes in anticipation. All eyes turn to a huge stone that stands outside the great circle. Finally, a thin beam of sunlight flickers over the horizon. As it reaches

Stonehenge, the top of the sun's disk seems to appear at the top of the stone.

The crowd gives a low sigh, for this is what the people came to see. This is what Stonehenge was built for—or so many think: to mark the spot of the midsummer sunrise. But there are many theories of why and how Stonehenge was built. And the greatest mystery of all is—who built it?

We know the name of the emperor who began the Great Wall of China. We know much about the ancient Egyptians who built the pyramids. Stonehenge may be older than the pyramids, and is certainly older than the Great Wall. But unlike the Egyptians and the Chinese, the Stonehenge builders had no written language. The only clues to their civilization lie in the awesome monument they built, and in the ground around Stonehenge.

First, let's take a look at what can be seen above ground. Set in the middle of a large, flat plain, Stonehenge stands out, visible for miles around. Approaching it, a visitor soon sees that these huge stones could not have been placed here through some natural process like a flood or a glacier. Human beings put them here, in a way that someone planned carefully.

Stonehenge is more than just a single circle of big stones. It is a very complex structure. Even though many of the stones have fallen over the

centuries, it is still possible to envision what it must once have looked like.

The outer stones are about thirty feet high and six feet wide. They were originally set up in pairs with a third stone on top, forming a "doorway" that today's archaeologists call a trilithon. When complete, Stonehenge had fifteen trilithons. The capstones on top were curved and placed end to end so that the entire structure formed a nearly perfect circle.

The great circle of trilithons is only part of Stonehenge. Within the outer circle (called the Sarsen Circle) is a second circle of smaller stones. They look a bit like tombstones, though each one weighs from four to seven tons. They are made of bluestone, a different material from the gray sarsen stones of the outer circle.

Walk past the bluestone circle toward the center, and you will see more huge trilithons made of sarsen stone. Some remain standing, but others are toppled and broken. Some individual stones weigh as much as fifty tons. Originally, five trilithons stood here, forming a U. The open end of the U faced roughly northeast—in the direction of the midsummer sunrise in England.

Within this U are more small bluestones. Near the center of the structure is a single large stone on its side, called the Altar Stone. Earlier investigators thought it was used as an altar for sacrificing animals, or perhaps even humans.

This part of Stonehenge—the Sarsen Circle and everything within it—is about 100 feet (30 meters) in diameter. Though it is the most impressive part of Stonehenge, it is just a small part of what the ancient builders made here.

They may have begun with just a circle of earth. Walk farther out from the stone circle, and you find it. Though the centuries have partially worn it away, a mound of earth forms a larger circle around the stone part of Stonehenge. The circle is about 350 feet (110 meters) in diameter. It has a gap in it—forming a "doorway"—facing northeast. Just outside the doorway, slightly to the right, is a single large stone, called the Slaughter Stone. This name was also given by earlier investigators who believed that Stonehenge was a place of sacrifice. Today it is believed that the Slaughter Stone was once part of a pair. Marks in the earth show that another stone stood alongside it, but no one knows what happened to it.

At the doorway begins a long "avenue" marked by banks of earth on either side. About 110 feet (33 meters) down the avenue is the last of the stones of Stonehenge. It is a huge boulder called the Heel Stone. The Heel Stone got its name because it has a small indentation on its side. An ancient legend tells that the devil threw the giant stone at a holy monk, catching him on the heel.

The avenue continues for about two miles

(3.2 kilometers) until it reaches the River Avon. And there, we think about the first puzzle of Stonehenge: How did these gigantic stones get here?

THE SOURCES OF THE STONES

One of the earliest people to write about Stonehenge had an answer that really belongs in the Fiction Files (and you'll read more about it there). Writing in the year 1136, the historian Geoffrey of Monmouth said that Merlin, the magician of King Arthur's court, brought the stones from Ireland, using magic.

People loved Geoffrey's tales of Merlin and Arthur and the Knights of the Round Table. But scientists of later centuries looked around for a better answer.

In 1580, William Lambarde, an English geographer, found stones of the same type as Stonehenge's big sarsen stones, at Marlborough, about eighteen miles from Stonehenge. Lambarde assumed that if enough workers put their backs to the task, they could have dragged the stones overland to Stonehenge. "Especially," he wrote, "if a prince be the paymaster."

Another writer claimed that Marlborough was originally called Merlin's Bury (or hiding place), and that Merlin's castle once stood there. So those who wanted to believe the tales of magic could still think that Merlin shaped the stones in his workshop.

The source of the smaller bluestones remained a mystery until our century. In the 1920s, H. H. Thomas of the British Geological Service found similar bluish stones in the Prescelly Mountains in Wales. But the Prescelly Mountains are 135 miles northwest of Stonehenge. That was very far for teams of workers to drag four-ton stones, even if many people put their backs to the task.

Around 1950, the master detective of Stonehenge took on the problem. He is Richard J. C. Atkinson, a brilliant archaeologist who has solved many of the Stonehenge mysteries during a lifetime of work.

Atkinson believes that the bluestones could have been brought to Stonehenge on canoes. Archaeologists have found remnants of dugout canoes made by Stone Age people in Britain. Atkinson drew up a route that followed the coast from the Prescelly Mountains to the mouth of the River Avon. From there, they could come upriver to the end of the long "avenue" that leads directly to Stonehenge.

Like many of the archaeologists you will read about in this book, Atkinson is a practical man. He wasn't content with sitting in a library, dreaming up theories. He tested his idea by building three canoes and lashing them together. In the summer of 1954, he loaded this canoe-raft with a concrete replica of a Stonehenge bluestone and floated it on the Avon

River. He recruited a crew of four high school
boys, who used poles to move the canoe up and
down the Avon. The builders of Stonehenge
could have brought the bluestones by water.

HOW WERE THE STONES MOVED OVER LAND?

But part of the journey had to be overland,
first from the Prescelly Mountains to the sea-
shore and later, up the avenue from the Avon
River to Stonehenge. Was it possible for Stone
Age people to move such huge stones on land?
How many people would it take?

Once again, Atkinson turned to his volunteer
schoolboys. He used thirty-two of them to drag
a wooden sledge loaded with the bluestone replica along Salisbury Plain. This sledge resembled a land raft, with ropes attached to drag it
forward.

Atkinson knew that the ancient people who
built Stonehenge had not discovered the wheel
and probably had no work animals to help
them. But he thought of another possible
method using the sledge. His schoolboys placed
the sledge on logs and used them as rollers. One
group of schoolboys walked behind the sledge,
picking up the rollers that the sledge had passed
over and moving them to the front of the
sledge. In this experiment, twenty-four boys
could move the sledge easily.

That seemed to solve the problem of moving
the bluestones. But what about the much larger

sarsen stones? Some of them were seven times as heavy as the bluestones. Though Stonehenge is only eighteen miles from Marlborough, there is no direct river route, and the land route is blocked by rivers and high hills.

Atkinson looked at the map and drew up a winding route twenty-four miles long, avoiding obstacles. Step by step he showed how the gigantic sarsen stones could have been moved.

Because the sarsens were so much heavier than the bluestones, the equipment would have to be much stronger. A single roller to support the sledge would weigh 300 pounds—and it would be only one of many rollers. Ropes to pull the sledge could have been braided from animal hides, but they would have to be very long so that hundreds of people could pull them.

Atkinson calculated that it would take 1,500 people to move just one stone along his twenty-four-mile route, and that it would take them at least seven weeks. The job of moving all the sarsen stones would have taken at least ten years.

However, it is doubtful that 1,500 people could be spared for such a task. From what we know about Stone Age society, most people had to work growing or hunting food in order to stay alive. There was no extra time for people to build something as massive and time consuming as Stonehenge. And of course, there

were far fewer people living in Stone Age Britain than there are today.

Yet somehow they did it. How long could the building of Stonehenge have taken? That is one of the questions that Atkinson turned to next. The answers he found made Stonehenge seem an even more awesome achievement.

THE STAGES OF BUILDING STONEHENGE

Atkinson started with the great earthen circle that surrounds Stonehenge. In reality, it is a twin circle of earth with a ditch in between, although silt has virtually filled in the ditch. Because it is a nearly perfect circle, it must have been laid out carefully before work began. Atkinson thinks the people who dug it attached a 175-foot long rope (made of twisted vines or skins) to a stake in the center of the circle. Workers moved the end of the rope around the planned circle, leaving some kind of trace to mark the place where people were to dig.

This is the only possible method ancient people could have used to mark off such a huge, perfect circle. But it could *not* have been done if there were any large rocks within the earth circle to block the rope. Thus, Atkinson felt that the circle must have been dug before the bluestones or sarsens were set up. This part of Stonehenge he called Stonehenge I.

Atkinson began to dig into the chalk soil of the twin circles. He found many objects, in-

cluding pickaxes made from the antlers of deer and shovels made from the shoulder blades of cattle. Fragments of pottery and various other animal bones were also inside the bank.

Gradually, a picture of the builders of this first Stonehenge emerged. Using bone tools, men and women hacked away at the chalky soil, intent on marking off this gigantic circle, as wide as a football field. The work was hard and long, and the people stopped to drink from pottery cups and eat cooked deer, sheep, or pigs, tossing the bones aside as they went back to work.

What was the circle for? Some archaeologists have suggested that it was a meeting place used for trade fairs or religious rites. There may have been a wooden structure inside, but if so, all traces of it have been lost.

Just inside the earthen circle are fifty-six regularly spaced pits that have been filled in with earth different from that in the surrounding area. They are called the Aubrey holes, because they were first noticed by John Aubrey, a seventeenth-century investigator of the Stonehenge mystery. When Atkinson dug up these pits, he found cremated human bones in some of them. As you will read in the Fiction Files, this may confirm an ancient legend that Stonehenge was a burial place for heroes.

But it was more than that. For we know that even at this first stage, the builders made a break

in the mound—marking the place where people gathered inside could have seen the midsummer sunrise. For generations, the people who lived in the surrounding area may have gathered there to see the sun rise on the longest day of the year.

Many ancient peoples worshipped the sun. They knew that crops grew in summer, when the sun was warmest, providing them with food to last them through the long winter. They prayed that the sun-god would continue to bless them. Midsummer day was commonly a time for celebration and thanksgiving—as it still is in some countries. Almost certainly, Stonehenge began as a place to honor the sun.

Scientific examination of the bones found inside the earthen ditch showed Atkinson that Stonehenge I was built around 5,000 years ago, around 3,000 B.C. This is slightly before the first pyramids were built, far away in Egypt.

THE STONES ARRIVE

Around 800 years after Stonehenge I, a new phase of building began. The builders of Stonehenge II built the "avenue" leading from the Avon River and brought eighty-two bluestones from the Prescelly Mountains. They began to set up the bluestones in two circles inside the earthen circle.

The first sarsen stones also appeared during the building of Stonehenge II. These are known

as the station stones, and they were placed just inside the earthen circle, to form a rectangle. (Only two of them remain today, but marks in the ground show where the others were.) Atkinson thinks the builders stretched ropes from each stone to make two diagonal lines across the circle. The point where the lines crossed was the center of the new bluestone circles.

As you will read in the Fiction Files, other investigators think that the station stones had a more spectacular use. They may have been used to calculate certain positions of the sun and moon.

Stonehenge II seems to have been a failure. The two bluestone circles were never completed. At some point around 2000 B.C., work stopped. The bluestones were taken down. Some powerful figure—a Stone Age genius whose name is lost to history, unless there really was a man named Merlin—decided on a new plan for Stonehenge. And within a century, Stonehenge III was built.

This is the mightiest part of the structure, the part that has made Stonehenge a source of so much awe and mystery for thousands of years. The massive sarsen stones were brought from Marlborough. Forty-five of them made up the great sarsen circle, with its fifteen trilithons. Another fifteen sarsens went to make the five great trilithons arranged in a U in the center.

Very likely, two more sarsens were set up like pillars in the doorway.

The task of making Stonehenge III involved more than simply moving the stones from Marlborough. Each of the hard sarsen stones was evidently shaped to fit into its place in the grand design. And these builders had only stone tools to do the job. Bronze axes and hammers had not yet appeared in Britain.

One of the tools the builders used was a maul. This was nothing more than a hard, round rock. Holding it in one or both hands, a worker smashed it against one of the sarsens. Over time, each of the thirty upright stones in the circle was made smooth. Each one had to be the same size as its neighbors.

To find out how long the task of shaping the stones might have taken, a professional mason tried to do part of the job in 1924. Using a maul, it took him about an hour just to remove six cubic inches of rock from a similar sarsen stone. It was estimated that to complete the job of shaping all the rocks would have taken fifty masons—working ten hours a day, seven days a week—nearly three years. But how many people in a Stone Age culture could have been spared to do the job? Were there even fifty people in the vicinity of Stonehenge who had these skills?

After the rocks were shaped, they had to be moved into place. Visitors to Stonehenge today

find this the most amazing part of the job. It seems almost impossible that people without mechanical equipment could have raised these mammoth stones and put capstones weighing several tons on top.

Archaeologists think that trenches were dug in the ground to help hold the base stones in place. One side of the trench slanted toward the outer part of the circle. Teams of workers carefully used rollers to slide a stone into the trench. They could then hold it upright with ropes while the trench was filled in with smaller rocks and soil.

How did the builders then raise the capstones into place? Several methods have been suggested. The most likely way was with a platform of logs. The builders could have used a lever to raise one end of the stone and allow another log to be placed underneath. Then they would move to the other side and do the same thing. Bit by bit, a thirty-foot-high platform could be constructed, with the stone on top. The capstone could then be slid on top of the base stones. This sounds easy, but it would have taken a large work force to do the job.

The construction of the sarsen circle and the U inside it was an amazing achievement. But the builders were not finished. Over the next 900 years, they continued to add refinements to the structure. Two more circles of holes were dug inside the earthen circle. They are called the Y

and Z holes. They had no burial remains inside them, and were quickly filled in not long after they were dug. What were they for? As you will read in the Fiction Files, some of today's scientists have suggested a spectacular use for them.

Around 1100 B.C., the eighty-two bluestones of Stonehenge II—which had been stored somewhere for 900 years—were brought back. They were set up in the same pattern as the sarsen stones: a circle inside the sarsen circle, and a U inside the circle at the center. Stonehenge was finally complete.

What happened next? Nobody knows. No clear written record of Stonehenge appeared until the time of Geoffrey of Monmouth—more than 2,000 years after the building was completed. By then it was a wreck. How long was it used? What happened to the people who built it? And why did they build it?

It seems nearly unbelievable that a small group of Stone Age people could have built such an elaborate structure. Yet they did, devoting enormous time and effort to the project over at least twenty centuries. They must have had some purpose in mind. What was it? Who thought of it?

Some of the answers to these questions appear in the Fiction Files on page 1. As you will read there, some people believe that Stonehenge was

much more than a temple to worship the sun. And if their theories are correct, the people who built Stonehenge were the most amazing people in the world of their time.

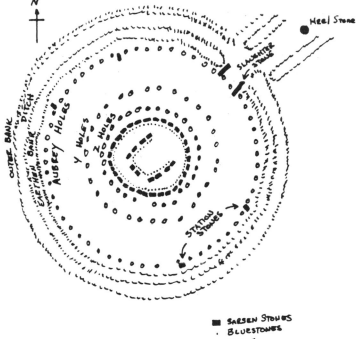

CHAPTER TWO: MYSTERIES OF ANCIENT AMERICA

No one really knows when the first human beings came to America. It was at least 12,000 years ago, but it may have been more than 30,000 years before that. We do know that the descendants of these ancient people developed a rich variety of cultures. Separated by enormous oceans from ancient civilizations of Asia, Africa, and Europe, they followed their own path of development.

When Europeans began to arrive in America, they conquered and destroyed many of the civilizations that they found. Today we are left with traces of the grandeur of the past—sculpture, pottery, jewelry, and fascinating monuments. Archaeologists and historians are still

trying to piece together the stories of the ancient Americans. We will look at only three of many possibilities.

THE OLMECS

The Olmec culture was the first great civilization in North America. It arose in what is today Mexico, near the southern coast of the Gulf of Mexico. People had been living there since at least 7000 B.C., raising crops such as corn, beans, squash, peppers, tomatoes, and avocadoes. They lived in small communities of wood and straw houses, wearing cotton clothing and making simple pottery.

Then around 1200 B.C., these early farmers suddenly developed the signs of a great civilization. Olmec artists began to produce fine sculpture and paintings. Large groups of people cooperated in building large earthen pyramids, probably lined with logs to keep them from collapsing. Open squares in front of the pyramids were used for religious ceremonies.

These included a sacred game played with a rubber ball. The rules of the game are unclear, but sculptures show the players knocking the ball with elbows and hips, and perhaps a bat. The game was deadly serious, for the losers were executed.

The Olmec leaders were priests whose knowledge of mathematics and engineering enabled them to direct the building of the pyramids. Ol-

mec priests devised the first calendar of Mexican civilization. It had a 365-day year, which meant that the Olmecs had made accurate observations of the sun over a long period. The priests used it to indicate when to plant and harvest the crops.

But the Olmec calendar was more complex than that. It dated back to an obscure event in the distant past. Some archaeologists say the starting year was equivalent to 3113 B.C. Olmec priests developed a number system that could pinpoint any given day from that year onward. The priests memorized certain dates that were important in the history of their people and transmitted them to the rest of the society.

The Olmecs also used picture symbols. Unfortunately, so few of the hieroglyphs survive that we do not know whether it was really a written language.

For over a thousand years, the Olmec people developed a more complex culture. The chief "god" of their religion was the jaguar, the fiercest animal they knew. Indeed, the Olmecs claimed to be related to jaguars. In the distant past a creature who could take the shape of a jaguar or a man united with a woman. She gave birth to a child that combined the features of a human and a jaguar. This creature became a favorite image of Olmec art. Jade sculptures often portray it as a baby, with indentations on the

top of the head for jaguar ears. These small sculptures often were buried with their owners.

Olmec leaders were often portrayed with another popular god—the fire bird or quetzal. In southern Mexico early Olmecs painted their leader with a headdress of quetzal feathers intertwined with jaguars.

Around 1200 B.C. the Olmecs built the first of their huge centers at today's San Lorenzo, near the modern city of Veracruz. Workers carrying earth built a raised surface 150 feet high. Atop this plateau, they raised smaller hills in a step-pyramid fashion.

San Lorenzo became the center of Olmec culture. It was not a city, for only priests and artists lived there. Other people came from nearby areas to trade and attend the religious ceremonies.

It was at San Lorenzo that the most awesome of the Olmec sculptures were first created. These were mammoth stone heads, carved from a single block of stone. At least seven were created from around 1200 to 900 B.C. The faces are stern and fearsome, and appear to be wearing helmets.

Around 900 B.C., the San Lorenzo site was destroyed. The great stone heads were carefully buried underground—perhaps to take away their power. Over the centuries erosion brought them to the surface again.

But the Olmec culture did not die with San

Lorenzo. Another line of rulers arose. Their power centered around what is today La Venta, on an island about eighteen miles upriver from the Gulf of Mexico. Here a new, even larger ceremonial center was built, covering about two square miles. It was dominated by a ridged cone of earth 130 feet high. It may have been shaped to look like a volcano. More colossal heads appeared, some weighing over 50,000 pounds.

At the height of the civilization, over 1,000 aristocrats, priests, and artists lived at the La Venta site. In the outlying areas lived another 10,000 people, growing the food that supported the population of the ceremonial center.

From La Venta, Olmec influence spread. Olmec traders carrying products and ideas traveled through today's southern Mexico and part of Central America. Other, smaller, ceremonial centers arose. The Olmec elite influenced the surrounding people in dress, religious beliefs, and scientific knowledge.

The Olmecs dressed in tunics and skirts made of cotton or other vegetable fibers. They loved to adorn themselves with jewelry of jade and polished stones. They wore such stones in their pierced ears. Bracelets and anklets adorned their arms and legs. Around their necks priests wore polished pieces of mirrorlike stone that may have been used to start fires in religious ceremonies.

Around 400 B.C., La Venta was destroyed in

as brutal a way as San Lorenzo had been. Again, the stone heads were defaced or buried—but no one knows who did it or why. A smaller Olmec center kept the old traditions alive for another 200 years. But gradually the jungle covered the great plazas and pyramids where Olmec priests once carried on their rites.

Other peoples of early America adopted some of the Olmec beliefs and knowledge. The cult of the jaguar-man spread to other areas of Mexico and Central America. The Maya adopted the Olmecs' calendar and developed their picture-writing into a more complicated written language. The sacred ball game was a part of the Aztec culture when the Spanish arrived, seventeen centuries after the fall of the Olmecs.

But the civilization of the Olmecs lay undiscovered in the jungles until the past century. Explorers, having heard tales of the lost temples of a vanished civilization, found the Olmec sites. Archaeologists are still trying to solve many of the puzzles that the Olmecs left—as you can read in the Fiction Files on page 19.

THE NAZCA LINES

If you visit the South American country of Peru, take a plane ride over the desert between the Pacific Ocean and the Andes Mountains. You will see an astonishing sight. On the flat, bare land below are huge pictures of animals,

birds, and plants. At least 1,500 years ago, ancient Americans made these pictures by clearing away the rocky surface to expose the light-colored soil.

There are many remarkable things about these pictures. But the most remarkable is this: they cannot be seen from the ground and were not discovered until an airplane pilot flew over the region in the 1920s and looked down. Because it almost never rains in this desert plateau, the pictures had remained undisturbed for fifteen centuries.

The Nazca Lines, as the pictures are called, occupy an area of over 200 square miles. It took hundreds of years to make them all. Millions of rocks had to be cleared away to expose the soil underneath. The rocks are carefully lined up in rows around the shapes.

Why would people go to such trouble to make pictures they could not have seen? As you can guess, many people have suggested answers to that question. But for now, let's take a closer look at the Nazca Lines and the people who probably made them.

The most spectacular lines form pictures of birds, reptiles, whales, a spider, plants, and some human figures as well. One clearly shows a monkey with a coiled tail—as large as a football field. Yet the nearest jungle where monkeys live is 200 miles away. Whales are a bit closer,

in the Pacific Ocean on the edge of the Nazca region.

Other lines form geometrical shapes such as triangles, quadrangles, spirals, and circles. Some are simply straight lines, sometimes parallel to each other, that run for miles. All the lines in these geometrical figures are as straight as a ruler. It would take modern surveyors a good deal of effort to draw these lines on such a large scale.

How could ancient people have drawn them so perfectly? Along some of the lines, remains of posts can be found, spaced at intervals of about one mile. Perhaps they were sighting stations for the artists who made the Lines.

Even today, no one lives in most of the desert area near the Lines. Nothing grows here, not even cactus. But the closest ancient Americans were a people called the Nazca. And the pottery they made, found in graves, is decorated with pictures like those in the desert. Scientists feel that the Nazca made the Lines.

Who were the Nazca people? They lived and flourished in the coastal region between the years 100 B.C. and A.D. 700. The Nazca decorated their pottery in rich earth colors of bronze red, ocher, cream, and brown. From the pottery we can see the Nazca concern with fertility of the earth and with their crops. This is not surprising, for the dryness of the region meant that farmers had to use all their skill to

grow enough food. The pottery showed many edible plants. One favorite was the jack bean, believed to be the first crop that Nazca farmers planted. Another food and fertility symbol was the peppino, a form of cucumber.

The Nazca worshipped the life force in all creatures and forms of nature. Their pottery depicted wild animals of many types. They particularly honored whales and condors, the huge predatory South American bird.

A more bloody pottery subject was the severed heads of captured enemies. The heads were taken not only as trophies but because the Nazca believed that the life force of each human resided in its head. Therefore, Nazca warriors set out to take as many heads of their enemies as possible. In temples devoted to whales and condors, a warrior cult used their captured human heads in religious rituals.

The Nazca buried their dead in richly woven cloaks. In this dry area, the corpses and their clothing were preserved like mummies. Modern scientists have found that Nazca healers sometimes practiced trepanning—cutting into the bone of the skull to reach the brain. Their patients survived, for the mummies' skulls show that the bone grew back again to fill the holes.

We know that the Nazca had a rich and sophisticated culture. What we do not know for sure is why they devoted so much effort to creating those mammoth pictures on the floor of

the nearby desert plateau. Read some of the possible answers in the Fiction Files on page 24, and see if you agree.

THE MOUND BUILDERS

The early English settlers of the United States were disappointed that they did not find great monuments from earlier native American civilizations. Farther south, the Spanish had found (and plundered) the great Aztec capital at Tenochtitlán and the rich Inca city of Cuzco. There were no great Indian cities like these in the original thirteen colonies.

But in the 1700s, many settlers moved across the Appalachian Mountains. In what became the states of today's Midwest, pioneers came upon mysterious earthworks. Some were cone-shaped mounds, varying in size from a few feet high to 100 feet above ground level. Other earthworks were elongated ridges that had been formed into shapes such as gigantic snakes, mythical birds, and human forms. Still other earthworks formed large or small enclosures or were flat-topped pyramids.

The settlers wondered about these earthen mounds. Who made them and why? When settlers questioned the Indians living nearby, they got no satisfactory answers. The Indians were no longer making the mounds, and settlers doubted that they ever did. As you will read in the Fiction Files, all sorts of theories were put

forth, trying to explain that someone other than the Indians built these mounds.

As the settlers continued to pour farther into today's United States, they found more of these mounds. Scientists today estimate that throughout the Ohio River valley alone, there were more than 10,000 separate earthworks. Others were found throughout the southern states and as far west as the Mississippi River. If all were the work of a single culture, these people had spread over a very large area.

One of the most interesting mounds is in southern Ohio, upriver from today's city of Cincinnati. Here is the Great Serpent Mound, shaped like a giant snake. Curving back and forth, it stretches for a quarter mile across the landscape. The snake's mouth is open, and it appears to be swallowing an egg-shaped object.

The largest of the mounds was at Cahokia, Illinois—just across the Mississippi River from modern St. Louis. It rose 100 feet high and its base enclosed an area of over fifteen acres—larger than the bases of the Egyptian pyramids. The mound ascended in several large steps. We know today that on the top of the mound was a temple that commanded a view of the settlements around. On its lower terrace stood the homes of the notables and high officials.

Experts today estimate that the Cahokia mound contains about twenty-two million cubic feet of earth. Because there were no draft

animals such as horses or oxen in ancient America, Cahokia was built one basket of earth at a time. Thousands of people who lived in a single community combined their labor to build it. More than eighty smaller mounds have been found nearby.

Though the white settlers were awed by such monuments, they had little respect for them. Farmers plowed many of them flat to make room for their crops. They sometimes found skeletons buried inside, along with a treasure trove of other objects. These included statues of wood, clay, and mica, some depicting people, animals, and birds. Soapstone pipes had bowls carved into the shape of birds and frogs. Sometimes the dead had been buried with copper and stone ornaments.

Henry Shetrone, a nineteenth-century archaeologist, described the grave of a young man and woman:

At the head, neck, hips and knees of the female and completely encircling the skeleton were thousands of pearl beads and buttons of wood and stone covered with copper; extending the full length of the grave along one side was a row of copper ear ornaments; at the wrists of the female were copper bracelets; copper ear ornaments adorned the ears of both, and both wore necklaces of grizzly-bear canines [teeth] and copper breastplates on the chest.

Rumors spread that treasures of gold had been found in some of the mounds. This set off a treasure hunt that destroyed many of them, but unlike the fabulous cities of Latin America, the mounds yielded little precious metal.

There were some people who regretted the mindless destruction of the mounds. At Marietta, Ohio, the townspeople enclosed several mounds in a park to be preserved. When trees covering the mounds were cut down, a local clergyman counted 463 rings in one stump. Since the tree had grown since the mound had been built, the date of the mound's construction must have been around the year 1300.

Thomas Jefferson, the nation's third president, was also fascinated by the mounds. He found one near his home at Monticello, one of the few that exist east of the Appalachians. Carefully he dug it up, finding three layers of skeletons, about a thousand in all. Jefferson wrote that the local Indians revered the mound. Only thirty years earlier, Indians had conducted some kind of religious ceremony there. To Jefferson, it was clear that the ancestors of the Indians were buried at the site.

Yet for a long time, people refused to accept that simple conclusion. Most Indians the settlers knew followed a simple way of life. They lived in a land of plenty that provided all that they needed. They drank from the clear rivers and hunted for food, or picked it where it grew

wild. Many lived in small settlements, growing their own food. Others stalked the animals of the forest and plain, wearing the hides of deer, beaver, or buffalo. These could not have been the people who built the mounds—or so the settlers thought.

This attitude was summed up by the American poet William Cullen Bryant in the early nineteenth century:

A race, that long has passed away,
Built them;—a disciplined and populous race.
. . .
These ample fields
Nourished their harvests, here their herds
    were fed,
When haply by their stalls the bison lowed,
And bowed his maned shoulder to the yoke.
. . .
The red man came—
The roaming hunter tribes, warlike and fierce,
And the mound-builders vanished from the
    earth.

With that belief in mind, many strange theories were offered as to the "real" identity of the Mound Builders. Who were the people who raised these earthworks and created the highest ancient civilization in the United States? You can read some answers in the Fiction Files on page 30.

CHAPTER THREE:
ATLANTIS: THE LOST CONTINENT

Atlantis is more than a lost civilization. It is a lost continent, said to have existed almost 12,000 years ago in what is today the Atlantic Ocean. Virtually all that we know about Atlantis rests on two documents that were written by the Greek philosopher Plato around the year 350 B.C. Ever since that time, people have searched for traces of the real Atlantis.

Plato did not write the way historians do. He presented his thoughts in the form of "dialogues," which are like stories in which several people discuss thought-provoking questions. Plato often puts his own opinions in the mouths of others, particularly his teacher Socrates. Because Socrates himself left no writings, it is dif-

ficult to tell whether he really said what Plato reports, or if Plato was using Socrates' great prestige to put across his own ideas.

The two dialogues in which Plato mentions Atlantis are called the *Timaios* and the *Kritias*. These titles are also the names of two of the people who are speaking in the dialogues. Others include Socrates and Hermokrates. As the *Timaios* begins, the four men are discussing the origins of the world. The character Kritias tells a story that was passed down from his own great-grandfather, who heard it from Solon, a Greek statesman.

Almost 250 years before Plato's story was written down, Solon traveled to Egypt. He met a group of priests who told him of Atlantis. As you see, Plato's account of Atlantis is already a story within a story within a story. Not the most reliable historical evidence!

The priests told Solon that Egypt had historical records that went back many thousands of years to the creation of the world. They said that Athens, the city-state in which Plato lived, had ruled a great empire, 9,000 years before his time. (That would have been around 11,600 years ago.)

But Athens had a rival. A second great empire, Atlantis, existed beyond "the Pillars of Hercules." These were two mountains at the Strait of Gibraltar, the place where the Mediterranean Sea meets the Atlantic Ocean. To Plato's

readers, this meant that Atlantis was some-where in the Atlantic.

The island of Atlantis was very large—bigger than "Africa and Asia combined"—though Plato had no idea how large either of those continents really were. The Atlanteans were great seafarers. They had traveled westward through smaller islands, reaching the "opposite continent" on the other side of the Atlantic Ocean.

The people of Atlantis turned eastward, and invaded the Mediterranean region. They spread across North Africa into Egypt and on the northern shore conquered parts of Italy as well. Atlantis thus threatened the empire of Athens.

The Athenians sent a great fleet to meet them. While the battle hung in the balance, a great earthquake and flood struck the world. The Athenian army and navy were destroyed, but a worse fate was in store for the people of Atlantis. The great worldwide earthquake and flood devastated their mighty island. "In a terrible night and day," Atlantis sank beneath the Atlantic Ocean. Plato adds that this disaster left the ocean filled with dangerous shoals that made it impossible for ships to venture out on it.

At this point in the *Timaios*, Kritias interrupts his story. He promises to tell more but prefers to listen first to Timaios's ideas about the creation of the world and the nature of the universe. These take up the rest of the *Timaios*.

Plato makes his readers wait until the next dialogue to hear more about Atlantis.

In the dialogue called *Kritias,* Plato has Kritias describe the founding of both Athens and Atlantis. When the gods divided up the world, they gave Athens to the goddess Athena. The sea-god Poseidon, appropriately, received Atlantis. Poseidon mated with Kleito, the daughter of a human couple who lived on Atlantis. Poseidon and Kleito had ten sons, half-human, half-god.

These ten became kings, dividing Atlantis and neighboring lands among themselves. Atlas, the eldest son, was chief king of Atlantis. His brother Gadeiros received Gadeira, which was in the land we call Spain. (Keep this in mind, for it has some significance to those who believe Atlantis really existed.)

Poseidon made a home for Kleito on a hill in Atlantis. To keep it safe, he surrounded it with rings of land and water. This was the foundation of the city of Atlantis, on the southern part of the island-continent. Later, the kings and their descendants built bridges and tunnels through the rings, and a canal cutting straight through the city. Kritias describes the fabulous wealth of Atlantis, whose buildings were decorated with gold, silver, ivory, and a metal (*oreichalkos*) that "glowed like fire." Every few years, the kings met in a great palace on the hill where Kleito had lived. They captured and sac-

rificed a bull, and made decisions on important matters.

Over time, the people of Atlantis fell into evil ways. Zeus, the chief god in the Greeks' mythology, decided to punish them to show his displeasure. He called the other gods together, "and when he had assembled them, he spake thus:"

What did he say? Nobody knows, for the *Kritias* that Plato wrote stops there. Scholars say that Plato intended to write three dialogues about the origins of Athens and Atlantis and the climactic battle between the two empires. But he apparently did not finish the second one, and never began the third.

MODERN FACTS AND PLATO'S STORY

You have probably already noticed an interesting fact about Plato's account of Atlantis. He tells of a continent on the other side of the Atlantic Ocean—even though he was writing eighteen centuries before Columbus crossed the ocean. Those who believe in Plato's story of Atlantis point to this as evidence that it was true. For unless the Atlanteans really reached North or South America, how would Plato have known about this continent?

However, Plato may simply have drawn on the Greeks' general ideas of the world. They knew the world was a round globe, but they thought the center of it was the Mediterranean

Sea. From firsthand experience, or from reliable reports from such seagoing neighbors as the Phoenicians, they knew of the lands surrounding the Mediterranean. They grouped these lands into three continents—Europe to the north, Africa to the south, and Asia to the east. However, the Greeks didn't know the full extent of any of these three continents—just those parts nearest the Mediterranean.

Surrounding all three continents, the Greeks thought, was a great ocean. They knew the entrance to it was at the Pillars of Hercules. And somewhere beyond that, they thought, was an "outer continent" that in turn encircled the Ocean. Plato could well have thought that the people of Atlantis had reached this outer continent, supposedly an uninhabited land.

Believers in Atlantis have pointed to other details of Plato's story. One is his report that the sinking of Atlantis created shoals (banks of sand just beneath the water) that made it difficult for ships to cross the Ocean. Some writers have identified these shoals as the Sargasso Sea. This is a part of the Atlantic Ocean where huge amounts of seaweed float on or near the surface. Legends have told of ships sinking after being caught in the seaweed, but these stories have been disproved.

Remember, too, Plato's claim that one of the ten kings of Atlantis ruled over Gadeira. This might refer to the Spanish seaport of Cádiz,

earlier called Gadir. It is probably the oldest settlement on the Iberian peninsula. Archaeologists think it was founded by the Phoenicians, but some of the people of Atlantis may have been there first.

Are there any other traces of the Atlanteans? Consider the Basques, a distinct group of people who still live near the northern coastline of Spain and on the border of France and Spain. Their language is unrelated to any other known tongue. Scientists still puzzle over the origins of the Basques and their language. Could they be descendants of the Atlanteans?

Even more mysterious are the people known as the Guanches. They were living on the Canary Islands, just off the northwest coast of Africa, when Spanish explorers arrived there in the fifteenth century. The Guanches did not resemble Africans—they had blue or gray eyes and light-colored hair. Where did they come from?

One more interesting fact about the Canary Islands. How do you think the islands got their name? If you guessed from the islands' birds, you were wrong. In Latin, the word for dog is *canis*. Roman writers named the islands Canaria because many large dogs lived there. Later, the Spanish found not only dogs but also sheep and cattle. Large mammals like these are not usually found on islands, unless the islanders had some contact with mainland areas. Obviously, the Guanches had brought these animals

from whatever place they had lived in before. Atlantis?

One more scientific fact may tie in with Plato's story. Plato's dialogues about the origins of the world did not come near to the truth about the great age of the earth. Today's scientists believe it was created about 4.5 billion years ago. The first humans did not appear until 1.3 million years ago. At that time, the world's climate was much colder than it is today. Huge sheets of ice, called glaciers, covered much of the northern hemisphere. In the United States, some of these glaciers reached as far south as St. Louis, Missouri. Gradually, as the earth warmed up, the glaciers began to melt. Geologists place the end of this ice age about 11,000 years ago.

Does that ring a bell? At about that same time, Plato says, Atlantis sank beneath the sea. We know that the melting of the glaciers did in fact raise the level of the world's seas. Of course, it did not happen in a night and a day. It was a very gradual process. But it may have raised the Atlantic Ocean high enough to cover a large island—if one was there.

These facts are all clues, but they do not prove the existence of Atlantis. If you want to read some of the elaborate theories that modern writers have offered about the "real" Atlantis, you will have to turn to the Fiction Files on page 37. The rest of the Fact Files will give you

the evidence that makes most of today's scientists believe that Atlantis never existed—at least as Plato described it.

THE BOTTOM OF THE ATLANTIC OCEAN

Human beings have always been fascinated by the sea. Many seafaring peoples have had a sea god, such as the Greeks' Poseidon or the Romans' Neptune. This god ruled over the kingdom of the sea—so mysterious because people did not know what lay beneath the waters.

Modern science has given us submarines and bathyspheres in which we can travel into this kingdom. We have tools like sonar, which uses sound waves to "see" into the depths of the oceans. Scientists have drawn maps that show what the Atlantic Ocean would look like if it had no water in it.

Running down the center of the ocean floor, from Iceland nearly to the coast of South America, is the Mid-Atlantic Ridge. This is a vast chain of undersea volcanoes. Part of this ridge juts above the water, forming the Azores Islands. The Azores are about 750 miles west of Portugal, just about where you might expect Atlantis to have been according to Plato's story.

However, when a Portuguese ship arrived in the Azores in 1427, its crew found no people living there. Since then, no trace whatsoever of any previous human settlement has been found in the Azores. No ruined buildings, no coins,

no pottery, no bones. Nothing to indicate that this might once have been the homeland of the people of Atlantis.

Indeed, on either side of the Mid-Atlantic Ridge, the ocean floor slopes downward to depths of more than two miles beneath the surface. Scientists have sent underwater cameras to the ocean bottom and taken samples of the soil there. They found nothing to indicate that the floor of the ocean had been disturbed for tens of thousands of years—long before Atlantis was said to have been destroyed by earthquakes and flood.

We do know that such disasters have occurred in the past. As recently as 1883, a volcano exploded on the island of Krakatau (also known as Krakatoa) in Southeast Asia. The explosion completely destroyed the island—the sound alone was heard 3,000 miles away. It also caused a tidal wave that drowned tens of thousands of people on nearby islands. The plume of ash and smoke from the explosion drifted around the earth several times, causing cold weather and overcast skies throughout the world.

Yet Krakatau was only a small island. If a volcanic explosion large enough to devastate a continent-sized island occurred only 12,000 years ago, it would have left traces that could still be found, not only on the ocean floor but on land areas such as the coasts of Europe and America. And scientists have found no such telltale signs.

MOVING CONTINENTS

Recent scientific ideas about the formation of the world's continents also tend to disprove the idea of Atlantis. In the 1920s, Alfred Wegener, an Austrian scientist, suggested that the continental areas of the world were once part of a single land mass. Over millions of years, they have gradually drifted apart.

Later scientists developed this idea into the tectonic-plate theory that is generally accepted today. If you haven't yet studied it in science class, look at a map of the world. You will see that the east coast of South America seems to fit into the west coast of Africa, like pieces in a giant jigsaw puzzle. Scientists have found evidence that Brazil and the southwest coast of Africa once were joined together. In fact, the granite plates on which the continents rest are still moving apart—at the rate of about one inch a year.

Similarly, scientists think that North America was once connected to northern Africa and Europe. The Mid-Atlantic Ridge is the dividing line. If this is true, then there would have been no room for Atlantis between them.

In fairness to those who believe in Atlantis, we must add that North America and Europe don't fit quite so neatly together as South America and Africa. Moreover, the tectonic-plate theory also holds that continents can rise and fall.

THE ARCHAEOLOGISTS

Another argument against the existence of Atlantis is offered by archaeologists. They have unearthed the remains of many ancient civilizations in both the Mediterranean and the Americas. But they have found nothing that might have come from Atlantis.

What kind of evidence are they looking for? As Charles J. Cazeau and Stuart D. Scott point out in their book on ancient mysteries, if Atlantis really existed, "something tangible . . . pottery, a marble statue, inscriptions in a distinct language, rings, or other decorative objects" would have turned up in one of the civilizations that existed at the same time as Atlantis.

The date given by Plato for Atlantis—about 9500 B.C.—was quite a long time before the great civilizations of Sumer and Egypt arose. The world's oldest known city, Jericho, was built around 8000 B.C. Athens was probably not founded until around 4000 B.C., yet in Plato's story the Athenian empire existed at the same time as Atlantis.

Plato was not necessarily wrong if he merely exaggerated the age of Atlantis. Nevertheless, a civilization that was advanced enough to send a navy into the Mediterranean would certainly have left some traces of its existence. Yet archaeologists have found nothing that they can point to and say, "This came from Atlantis."

Or have they? Now it is time to turn to the Fiction Files on page 46 and read the arguments in favor of Atlantis. You will find some amazing theories, linking Atlantis to several of the other mysterious civilizations discussed in other chapters of this book.

CHAPTER FOUR:
THE RIDDLE OF MINOAN CIVILIZATION

According to Greek mythology, Poseidon, the god of the sea, sent King Minos of Crete a beautiful white bull. It was intended to be sacrificed to the gods. But when the beautiful white animal stepped from the waves, greedy King Minos decided to keep it. Poseidon, angered, decided on a terrible revenge.

He caused the wife of Minos, Pasiphae, to fall in love with the beautiful animal. In order to satisfy her unnatural passion, she enlisted the help of an exile from Athens, Daedalus. He built for her a large wooden cow. Hidden in this contraption, Pasiphae visited the bull. From the union of Pasiphae and the bull was born a terrible monster called the Minotaur. It

had the head of a bull and a body of a human. Daedalus built a maze of many rooms called the Labyrinth to imprison the creature.

Later, King Minos sent his son to Athens to compete in athletic games held in that city. That young man swept to victory in the contests. This aroused such envy among the Athenians that they killed the youth. When word of his son's death reached King Minos, he assembled an army that laid siege to Athens. Helped by disease and drought, Minos defeated the Athenians. He demanded from them a tribute of seven young men and seven women each year. These youths would come to his castle at Knossos in Crete and be eaten by the Minotaur.

Theseus, a son of the Greek king, offered himself as a sacrifice on one of these tribute missions. When Theseus arrived at Knossos, King Minos's daughter fell in love with him. She decided to help him by supplying a ball of thread to enable him to find his way out of the Labyrinth. Theseus entered the Labyrinth, letting the thread unravel behind him as he made his way through its many rooms. When he arrived at the center, he slew the Minotaur and followed the trail of thread to escape.

Through the ages, this story was believed to be only a myth. Even the Greeks who retold the tale did not know that it was based on fact. It was not until the end of the nineteenth century

that the origin of the myth would be discovered.

Sir Arthur Evans, an English archaeologist, had long been inspired by Greek history. He was thrilled by the discoveries of the German archaeologist Heinrich Schliemann. Schliemann believed that the stories of the Trojan War told by the legendary poet Homer were true. He dug up a site in modern-day Turkey that proved to be the location of the ancient city of Troy. This discovery led Evans to think that other Greek myths might also have factual origins.

Arthur Evans's specialty was ancient languages. He was fascinated by strange clay tablets he bought in a Greek antiques shop. The tablets were covered with what appeared to be writing. But the writing resembled no language Evans had ever seen before, not classical Greek or anything else. The antiques dealer told Evans that the tablets were from Crete. Evans went there, looking for more.

Crete is a large island in the Mediterranean, south of the Greek peninsula. At Knossos, a spot on the northern coast, Evans found a large mound that looked promising. He purchased the land and began to dig. What he unearthed over a twenty-five-year period was a hitherto unsuspected civilization—the earliest in Europe.

Under the mound, Evans found a huge palace with dozens of rooms. The entire building cov-

ered six and a half acres. Within this multitiered stone structure were royal apartments, shrines, production rooms for pottery, and workshops for other crafts.

The Knossos palace was a whole world unto itself. Some rooms held altars that were used for sacrifice. Others were storerooms filled with goods. They held hundreds of large jars, called *pithoi*. The pithoi had once been used for storing olive oil, honey, grain, wine, and figs—all products of the island. Open courtyards in the palace were large enough for crowds to gather to watch contests and games.

The royal family and their servants lived here in lavish splendor. The Minoans had the best plumbing of any people up to modern times. Private rooms included toilets and bathtubs. Minoan engineers showed their skill by constructing a series of interlocking pipes that brought water to the palace and took wastes away.

The palace was clearly a cultural and religious center as well as a seat of royal power. As room after room unfolded in an intricate pattern, Evans began to think that he had found the Labyrinth of Greek mythology. One immense room of the palace held a large chair, perhaps the first throne in European history. In remembrance of King Minos, Evans gave the name *Minoan* to the civilization he discovered.

The Minoans showed a highly refined artistic

talent. The archaeologist's spade uncovered hundreds of frescoes, or wall paintings. Some showed men dressed in short kilts with tight waists. Bare-chested, the slender men had long, flowing locks of hair. On their feet were high-laced boots. The women were stunning. Wasp-waisted in dresses that exposed their breasts, they let their long hair fall freely behind them. In fact, the women looked so chic that one of the diggers exclaimed, "They are Parisians!"

Other frescoes showed dolphins jumping above the waves, flying birds, flowers, and scenes from both land and sea. This art is colorful and joyous, reflecting the peaceful and prosperous life of the Minoans.

Some of the most interesting wall pictures showed male and female youths playing with fierce-looking bulls. In one of these pictures, a young woman is holding a bull by the horns. A young man seems to be turning a somersault on the bull's back, and a second woman stands at the tail, apparently to catch the young man when he tumbles off. Could this game have some connection with the legendary bull of King Minos?

In the years after Evans's first discoveries, other archaeologists arrived in Crete. They found other palaces—not so grand as the one at Knossos—in other places on the island of Crete. Gradually, a picture emerged of the nature of the Minoan society.

The Minoans were a seafaring people. Replicas of their ships have been found. The skillful Minoan sailors traveled far from the island. The ships brought products from throughout the Mediterranean, Egypt, and the Middle East. In return, the Minoans traded their finely wrought pottery, as well as olive oil and wine.

Sizable towns grew up around the palaces. These included two- and three-story houses that might have as many as a dozen rooms. The ceilings were low, indicating that adult Minoans were only about five feet tall. The town around Knossos held about 40,000 people. Archaeologists estimate that the population of the whole island was a quarter of a million—making it one of the most densely populated areas of the world at that time.

The Minoans' sea power apparently made them strong enough that they did not fear invaders. Unlike any of the ancient cities of the Middle East, none of the towns around the Minoan palaces had a defensive wall around it. Minoan art did not depict wars or battle scenes. This lack of interest in warlike behavior apparently indicates that the Minoans did not usually fight among themselves.

There may have been no need to fight, for Crete seems to have been a land of plenty. The Minoans ate bread made from wheat and barley flour and the fruits of the orchards of the countryside. But they were clearly health and diet

conscious. They kept in shape by practicing athletic games and acrobatics. Both men and women battled each other in boxing contests.

The Minoan sport of jumping or somersaulting over charging bulls required extensive training. Wild bulls were captured and trained for these spectacles. The acrobats practiced on tamer animals. These competitions attracted large crowds, and the palace complexes included large arenas where the games took place.

But bull jumping was also a religious celebration. After the performance, the bull was sacrificed to the mother goddess, the most important Minoan deity. She appears on many religious objects. Sometimes she is shown with a young man who may represent her son. In other scenes, the mother goddess is holding snakes wrapped around her body. Minoans may have regarded snakes as threatening creatures from the underworld. As we will see, the Minoans had good reason to fear the power of the earth.

The Minoans had no special temples for religious rites. Instead, altars and images of the goddess were part of the palace complexes. Some rites may have taken place outdoors and in caves, for the goddess appears to have ruled over the natural world. Because she controlled the weather, it was in her power to grant good crops. Men and women danced before her im-

age and offered sacrifices such as birds on her altars.

The Minoan civilization flourished from about 2000 B.C. to around 1375 B.C. Carbon dating places Minoan artifacts in that period. In addition, the trade products found on Crete match those made in ancient Egypt, Syria, Palestine, and Mesopotamia during this time.

Confirmation for these dates also comes from Egyptian tomb paintings and written records. The Egyptian frescoes show a foreign people bringing gifts in pots shaped like bulls' heads. These people, called the Keftiu, came from "the isles in the midst of the sea." The Keftiu look very much like the Minoans' pictures of themselves.

We know that the Minoans founded colonies in other places around the Mediterranean. One of these was on the island of Thera (now Santorin), about seventy miles north of Crete. In the 1960s, a Greek archaeologist unearthed pottery and wall paintings on Santorin that clearly were made by people of the Minoan civilization. These were much better preserved than the ones on Crete, and provided more information about the Minoan civilization.

One of the paintings shows two boys boxing. They wear gloves—the first time in human history that this kind of protective hand covering appears in a picture. Today's heavyweight champions wear gloves that are not much differ-

ent from those used by Therans 3,500 years ago.

In the center of Thera was an active volcano. When the people feared that it was about to erupt, most of them fled the island. When the volcano blew up, it covered the towns of Thera with molten lava. They were preserved forever, just as the Roman city of Pompeii was when Mt. Vesuvius erupted in the first century A.D.

As you will read in the Fiction Files, the destruction of Thera holds an important clue to the sudden and mysterious disappearance of the Minoans.

Crete, the homeland of the Minoans, lies in an earthquake zone. Devastating earthquakes swept the island around 1600 B.C. These destroyed the palaces and may have led to unrest among the people. For the first time, signs of fighting among the towns can be seen. The Knossos palace group seems to have escaped serious damage from the earthquake. As a result, Knossos emerged as the dominant center of Minoan civilization.

The other palaces were rebuilt. For another 100 to 150 years a brilliant culture flourished. Around 1450 B.C., a new style of art appeared—more formal and less joyous than the earlier frescoes. The towns declined in size. The people appear to have scattered into pastoral settlements.

Finally, the palace of Knossos was destroyed

in a great fire. Arthur Evans found traces of it when he first began digging. The pithoi (jars) were blackened by smoke, and charred wooden pillars had fallen, causing the stone ceilings and walls to collapse.

Once masters of the Mediterranean Sea, the Minoans disappeared from history with only the Greek myth as a trace of their existence. Their brilliant culture fell from prosperity to destruction in a very short period of time. What really happened? Turn to the Fiction Files on page 49 for some theories—and some additional mysteries.

CHAPTER FIVE:
EASTER ISLAND: THE
WALKING STATUES

E aster Island is one of the most isolated spots in the world. It lies in the Pacific Ocean, about 2,000 miles west of the coast of South America and 1,000 miles east of the nearest inhabited island. The island is only about eleven miles long and fifteen miles wide. Yet it contains the traces of a civilization that has mystified scientists for centuries.

The gigantic stone statues of Easter Island are almost as well known as the Great Sphinx of Egypt. Some stand buried up to their necks on the hillside of an extinct volcano. Others, as tall as thirty-five feet, lie along the beaches of the island, toppled from the massive stone bases on which they once stood. All look alike, with

sharp, chiseled features and empty eye sockets. A closer look reveals slender arms carved against the sides of the figures, tapering to long-fingered hands. None of the statues has legs. Each one, when it was standing, also was topped with a cylinder of red stone that did not match the gray volcanic rock from which the statues were carved.

As we will see, these statues are only a part of the Easter Island mystery. Other carvings, of both wood and stone, have long been hidden in caves underneath the island. Few of them resemble the giant statues — many show very different artistic influences. Also, wooden tablets with pictographic symbols on them show that the islanders once had a written language. Yet no one living on the island today can read it.

The islanders' legends are part of the mystery. They tell of a great king and his brother arriving by sea from the east hundreds of years ago. These were the ancestors of the "long-ears" who ruled the island and made the great statues (which do have long earlobes). Island tradition strongly holds that the statues "walked" down the hill from the volcano and made their way to their stone bases on the beach.

Then another people arrived — the "short-ears." For perhaps 200 years, the two groups lived peacefully together. But then the short-ears rebelled. The long-ears hid behind a large

ditch filled with firewood. They set it ablaze to keep back the short-ears. But the short-ears overcame them and drove the long-ears into the burning ditch. Afterward, the short-ears toppled the great statues, which were images of long-ear kings.

For a long time, scientists refused to believe this tale. They found it difficult to explain how even one group of people reached this isolated island, much less two. But as you will read in the Fiction Files, a great modern scientist feels he can account for every part of the legend—even the fact that the statues walked.

EUROPEANS ARRIVE

For now, however, let's look at some of the earliest accounts of European explorers in the Pacific. They provide the first clues to the secrets of Easter Island.

Three ships commanded by a Dutch admiral named Jacob Roggeveen arrived on Easter Sunday in 1722. He gave the island the name it bears today, though the islanders called their home Te-Pito-o-te-Henua, or "the navel of the world."

A storm prevented Roggeveen's men from going ashore the first day. The next morning, from the deck of his ship, he saw some of the massive statues, which at this time were still standing. As the sun rose, the islanders lit fires at the base of the statues and knelt. They

bowed, raising and lowering their arms in the direction of the sun. To Roggeveen, it was clear that he was witnessing a religious ritual.

When he finally came ashore, Roggeveen noted that there were several types of people on the island. Some were dark, others were "quite white," and a few "reddish . . . as if somewhat severely tanned by the sun." The light-skinned people also wore plugs in their earlobes. These plugs stretched the lobes so much that when they were removed, the islanders could drape their earlobes over the tops of their ears.

Roggeveen and his crew noticed other un-usual things. Though plenty of fish swam in the waters off the island, the islanders did not seem to rely on them for food. Instead, they raised such crops as sweet potatoes, bananas, and sug-arcane. Otherwise, the island's vegetation was sparse, consisting mostly of grass and reeds. The islanders used the reeds to make small rafts, which held only a single person, who used his hands to paddle.

Like countless other visitors later, Roggeveen marveled at the large statues that he thought the islanders worshipped. He chipped a piece off one and decided that they were made from clay on the spots where they stood.

The islanders were friendly and seemed to have no weapons of any kind. They also had no fear of the Dutch sailors and frequently made off with their possessions. This habit led to a

fight, in which the Dutch used their muskets to kill about a dozen islanders.

Not a very good beginning, but the people of Easter Island would suffer far worse from the outsiders who came after Roggeveen. It would be nearly fifty years before other Europeans arrived.

By that time, Spain had colonized most of the western part of South America. In 1770, the Viceroy of Peru sent an expedition to look for the island that Roggeveen had reported. Led by Felipe Gonzalez y Haedo, the Spanish found conditions much the same as Roggeveen described. Most Easter Islanders did not resemble the Indians of mainland South America. Some were dark, but others "might very well pass for Europeans." Those of the lightest-skinned group had reddish hair.

However, the islanders grew crops that the Spanish recognized as native to South America, including sweet potatoes, gourds, and a type of reed called totora. Like many modern scientists, the Spanish could not explain how these plants came to Easter Island.

The Spanish made a list of some words in the islanders' language. A few resemble words of the Polynesian people, who populated many of the islands of the South Pacific. But many more bear no resemblance to any other known language. Furthermore, Captain Gonzalez found that the Easter Islanders had a system of writ-

ing, which no Polynesians had. The mystery of Easter Island deepened.

The next European visitor was the English captain James Cook. One of the greatest navigators of all time, Cook made three epic round-the-world voyages in which he mapped much of the Pacific for the first time. Cook's voyages were intended to gather scientific information, and his ships carried artists and scientists who made careful records of the people they encountered. On Cook's second trip, he sailed from west to east, the first European to cross the Pacific in that direction.

On March 11, 1774, Cook sighted an island. Three days later, he and some of his crew went ashore. Cook knew of the earlier visits by Roggeveen and Gonzalez. On seeing the "idols" that Roggeveen had described on the beach, Cook knew he must be at Easter Island.

Cook was ill at the time, and sent his first mate, Richard Pickersgill, ashore with other crew members and scientists. Certain things had changed since the Spanish had been there, only four years earlier. The islanders were now seen carrying weapons such as clubs and spears, though they did not threaten Cook's men with them. Furthermore, the island's population seemed far smaller than Cook expected from earlier accounts. He thought that only about 600 or 700 people lived there, although Roggeveen had reported several thousand.

In addition, the tallest islander was under six feet, even though the Spanish had insisted that some of the "white" islanders were as tall as six and a half feet. We know that the long-ears were still among the people, for Cook's artist William Hodges made drawings of them. The sketches show both men and women with elongated earlobes reaching almost to their shoulders. But according to Pickersgill, almost all the people were dark-skinned, with black hair, not red. Cook considered it likely that they were related to the Maoris of New Zealand and the Polynesians of Tahiti—both of whom he had seen. Cook recorded the Easter Islanders' words for numbers, which were quite similar to the numbers on Tahiti.

Had some major event happened between Gonzalez's visit and Cook's? Further evidence comes from Cook's observation that many of the statues were toppled from their pedestals and broken. No previous visitor noticed this. Weapons, a reduced population, mostly dark-skinned . . . could this have been the time when the short-ears rebelled against the long-eared rulers? Were the "white" islanders now dead or in hiding?

Cook made two other important discoveries. From the observations made by his men, he decided that the great stone statues were not worshipped by the people. They were not "idols,"

but rather, images of kings; Pickersgill collected a list of their names.

Furthermore, Cook's men obtained beautifully carved wooden statues, which look very different from the stone images. Cook brought some of them back to England. They have prominent rib cages and grotesque, frightening faces. One more piece in the Easter Island mystery.

After two days, Cook sailed on, never to return. A French ship arrived in 1786, finding that the islanders had prospered. About 2,000 of them lived there by that time. If some unexplained disaster had struck before Cook arrived, the island's people had recovered from it. The French left behind some corn seeds, fruit trees, pigs, goats, and sheep. The French hoped to help the islanders raise a greater variety of food, but a century later, no trace of the French gifts remained.

THE DESTRUCTION OF EASTER ISLAND'S CULTURE

During the nineteenth century, the people of Easter Island greatly regretted their "discovery" by the outside world. In 1805, a ship from the United States landed there and captured twelve men and ten women. The American captain needed slave laborers for a seal-hunting colony he intended to establish on a Chilean island. After three days at sea, the captain released the men from their chains. They imme-

diately jumped into the ocean and began to swim in the direction of their home island. They were left to drown, and the ship returned for more slaves.

After this experience, the islanders became fiercely hostile to any sailors who tried to land. However, the slave-gathering expeditions continued. The worst came in 1862, when a ship from Peru captured 200 islanders. Among them was the king, Kaimakoi, and his family. The long line of Easter Island royalty ended.

After a Catholic bishop protested the raid, about fifteen of the islanders were returned. But they had contracted a fatal disease, smallpox, and spread it to the other islanders. When a Catholic missionary arrived in 1864, he found that the island's society had been shattered. Without a royal family, the islanders had fought among themselves. The strong preyed on the weak. People stole whatever they could from each other. All of the great statues had been overturned.

Unfortunately, this missionary, Eugene Eyraud, set about destroying what was left of the islanders' culture. Though the people no longer paid any attention to the stone statues, they kept within their houses many of the small wooden figures that Captain Cook had seen. Eyraud concluded that these images of "male figures, fishes, birds, etc." were idols. He said, "I have occasionally seen the natives taking

these statues, lifting them into the air, making some gestures, and accompanying all of it with a sort of dance and an insignificant song. . . . I believe they do not know much about it. They do quite simply what they have seen their fathers do, without offering it any further thought."

Thus, Eyraud sought to stamp out this pagan "religion" by destroying the figures. When he discovered that the people also had a great many wooden tablets with writing on them, he ordered these burned as well. The damage he and the slave traders did was permanent. Though a few wooden tablets survived, no one can read them. The tradition and history of the people of Easter Island was preserved only by word of mouth, handed down from one generation to the next.

The first person to write down these traditions was a later missionary, Father Hippolyte Roussel. Roussel found that the islanders' first king was named Hotu. He had arrived by boat from the direction of the rising sun—the east. Hotu's descendants ruled the island until the last king was taken away by the slavers.

The early islanders believed in a god named Make-Make. Through him, the island chiefs received divine powers. They ordered the construction of the stone statues, called *moai*. After the islanders made stone platforms, called *ahu*s, for the *moai*, the kings commanded them to

walk, "and immediately they began marching and came to the place they occupy today."

After the statues stood on the stone slabs, the islanders raised the red "hats" onto the finished statues. They could have done this in much the same way as the Stonehenge people raised the capstones. They would pry up one end of the "hat" and push smaller rocks underneath it. Then they would repeat the process on the other side, moving the "hat" higher and higher until it could be slid onto the head of the statue. This would have required a great deal of effort. Why were the "hats" so important? You will learn in the Fiction Files.

The missionaries also noted the presence of two groups of people on the island. Some were dark-skinned, but others were "fairer, some almost white. Some had red hair." This contradicts Captain Cook's report that all the inhabitants were dark-skinned.

Another visitor, an English doctor named J. L. Palmer, first heard the story that the present-day islanders were descended from a *second* group of immigrants. When they arrived, the long-eared builders of the stone statues were in possession of the island. The second group adopted their religion. Palmer found many more of the strange wooden images, indicating that the islanders had hidden them when Eyraud tried to destroy them.

German archaeologists came in 1882 and

found the source of the stone used to make the great statues. It was the cone of an extinct volcano, Rano Raraku. The statues were carved from the hard volcanic rock here. The people who carved them used rocks sharpened into points and held in the hand. Many of these rock chisels were still lying on the ground.

The Germans found large circular pits on the rim of the volcano. Islanders told them that poles had once been placed in them. When the statues were built, ropes were tied to these poles to lower the statues into the valley below. There, they began to "walk." The Germans could not believe that the pits were used for this purpose, for they were about six feet in diameter. No trees close to that size grew on the island. Where could the people have gotten such poles?

The South American nation of Chile annexed Easter Island in 1888. Chile leased most of the island to a British company, which apparently used the land for raising cattle and sheep. The village where the people of the island then lived was fenced in. They were forbidden to leave their village without an official pass.

The Easter Islanders were helpless to prevent this final insult to them and their culture. A Chilean warship visited the island once a year to bring provisions for the British and make sure order was preserved. The Easter Islanders' spears were no match for modern weapons.

They tended their own fields, as they had for centuries. When other boats arrived with curious tourists or scientists, the islanders sold them more wooden statues, some of which were freshly carved.

Far away, in universities and museums, scientists continued to speculate on the origin of the Easter Islanders and their culture. They studied photographs of the few statues that still stood, imbedded in the earth, on the plain beneath the volcano. The other statues lay abandoned and toppled near the beaches. Occasionally, a tidal wave washed some of them into the sea.

Easter Island waited for a new discoverer, who would believe the ancient traditions of its people and find the answers to its mysteries. To find out who that man was, turn to the Fiction Files on page 60.

FACT INDEX

Altar Stone, 3
America, 18–30
Arthur, King, 5
Athens, 32, 33, 34, 35, 42, 45
Atkinson, J. C., 6–12
Atlantis, 31–43
  Atlantic Ocean and, 31, 32, 33, 35, 36, 39–40, 41
  Plato's story and, 31–39, 42
Atlas, 34
Aubrey, John, 10
Aubrey holes, 10
Avon River, 6–7, 11
Azores Islands, 39–40
Aztecs, 22, 26

Basques, 37
boxing, 50, 51–52
Bryant, William Cullen, 30

Cádiz, 36–37
Cahokia, Ill., 27–28
calendar, Olmec, 19, 22
Canary Islands, 37
Cazeau, Charles J., 42
Chile, 65–66
Columbus, 35
continents, moving of, 41
Cook, James, 59–61, 62, 64
Crete, 44, 45, 46, 48, 49, 51, 52
Cuzco, 26

Daedalus, 44, 45

earthquakes, 52
Easter Island, 54
  Chile's annexing of, 65–66
  Cook and, 59–61, 62, 64
  crops on, 57, 58
  destruction of culture of, 61–66
  European explorers and, 56–61
  legends of, 55–56, 60
Easter Island statues, 54–66
  red "hats" of, 55, 64
  religious worship of, 56–57, 60
  "walking" of, 55, 56, 64, 65

Egypt, Egyptians, 2, 11, 32, 42, 51
Evans, Arthur, 46–47, 48, 53
Eyraud, Eugene, 62–63

fire bird, 20
France, 37
frescoes, 48, 51, 52

Gadeira, 34, 36–37
Geoffrey of Monmouth, 5, 15
glaciers, 38
Gonzalez y Haedo, Felipe, 58, 59, 60
Great Serpent Mound, 27
Great Wall of China, 2
Guanches, 37–38

Hermokrates, 32
Hodges, William, 60
Homer, 46
Hotu, 63

ice age, 38
Incas, 26

jaguar, 19
Jefferson, Thomas, 29
Jericho, 42

Kaimakoi, 62
Keftiu, 51
Kleito, 34
Knossos, 45, 46–47, 48, 49, 52–53
Krakatau (Krakatoa), 40
Kritias, 32, 33, 34–35

Labyrinth, 45, 47
Lambarde, William, 5
La Venta, 21–22

Make-Make, 63
Maoris, 60
Marietta, Ohio, 29
Marlborough, 5, 12, 13
Maya, 22
Mediterranean Sea, 35–36, 42, 46, 51
Merlin, 5, 12

Mid-Atlantic Ridge, 39–40, 41
Minoan civilization, 44–53
 art of, 47–48, 49, 52
 Greek myths and, 44–46, 47, 48
 sports and games of, 47, 48, 50, 51–52
Minos, King, 44, 45, 47, 48
Minotaur, 44–45
moon, 12
Mound Builders, 26–30
 Cahokia mound built by, 27–28
 Indians as, 26–27, 29–30
 skeletons and treasures buried by, 28–29
Mt. Vesuvius, 52
mummies, 25

Nazca Lines, 22–26
Nazca people, 24–26
 pottery of, 24–25
Neptune, 39
New Zealand, 60

Ohio River valley, 27
Olmecs, 18–22
 religion of, 18, 19–20, 21, 22
 stone head sculptures of, 20, 21, 22

Palmer, J. L., 64
Pasiphae, 44
Phoenicians, 36, 37
Pickersgill, Richard, 59, 60, 61
Pillars of Hercules, 32, 36
pithoi, 47, 53
Plato, 31–39, 42
Polynesians, 58–59, 60
Pompeii, 52
Poseidon, 34, 39, 44
pottery, Nazca, 24–25
Prescelly Mountains, 6, 7, 11
pyramids, 2, 11, 18

quetzal, 20

River Avon, 6–7, 11
Roggeveen, Jacob, 56–57, 58, 59
Roussel, Hippolyte, 63

San Lorenzo, 20–21
Santorin (Thera), 51–52
Sargasso Sea, 36
Schliemann, Heinrich, 46
Scott, Stuart D., 42
Shetrone, Henry, 28
Socrates, 31–32
Spain, 34, 36–37, 58
Stone Age, 6, 7, 8–9, 13, 15
stone heads, 20, 21, 22
Stonehenge, 1–16, 64
 Altar Stone of, 3
 "avenue" of, 4, 11
 bluestones of, 3, 6, 7, 9, 11, 12, 15
 capstones of, 3, 14, 64
 Heel Stone of, 4
 moving of stones for, 7–9
 phases of building, 9–15
 sarsen stones of, 3–4, 5, 9, 11–14, 15
 Slaughter Stone of, 4
 sources of stones in, 5–7
 station stones of, 12
 twin circle around, 9–10
 Y and Z holes of, 14–15
Strait of Gibraltar, 32
Sumer, 42
sun, 19
 Stonehenge and, 2, 11, 12, 16

Tahiti, 60
tectonic-plate theory, 41
Tenochtitlán, 26
Thera (Santorin), 51–52
Theseus, 45
Thomas, H. H., 6
Timaios, 32, 33
trepanning, 25
trilithons, 3, 12
Trojan War, 46

Vesuvius, Mt., 52
volcanoes, 40, 52, 65

Wales, 6
Wegener, Alfred, 41

Zeus, 35

A tablet containing some of the mysterious writing that was developed by the Easter Islanders. No one alive today can read the messages on the stone tablets. *(Courtesy of Ladeco Airlines)*

Two of the huge pictures cut into the surface of the
Nazca Plain in Peru. One resembles a spider and the
other a hummingbird, which was worshiped by
some early peoples of South America. Notice that
each picture is made from a single line, starting and

ending at the hummingbird's beak and one of the
spider's legs. Possibly people walked along the path
made by the lines as a religious ritual. *(Courtesy of
the Peru Tourist Office)*

These massive stone heads stand on the hillside of the volcano at the center of Easter Island. The heads were carved in the crater of the volcano and then, according to Islander legend, they "walked" down the hill to their resting places. *(Courtesy of Ladeco Airlines)*

One of the Olmec stone heads that have been found on the jungle floor in the Yucatan Peninsula of Mexico. This particular head seems to show a man with features typical of African people. Could it mean that Africans crossed the Atlantic to the Americas long before Columbus? *(Courtesy of the Mexican Ministry of Tourism)*

Part of the Minoan Palace at Knossos, on the Mediterranean island of Crete. Destroyed by earthquake and fire, it remained hidden until Arthur Evans began to excavate it late in the nineteenth century. The entire palace structure covers more than six acres. A great civilization flourished here around thirty-seven centuries ago. *(Courtesy of the Greek National Tourist Organization)*

This picture of a young woman is one of the frescoes painted on the interior walls of the Knossos
palace. When archaeologists uncovered her face,
they called her La Parisienne, because she seemed
as chic and modern-looking as the fashionable
women of modern Paris. The knotted hair at the
back of her head may indicate that she was a priest-
ess. *(Courtesy of the New York Public Library)*

Visitors at Stonehenge today. Note the bump, or tenon, on top of the sarsen stone at right. The capstone that once rested on top had a hollow cavity, or mortise, that fit over the tenon. The smaller dark stone just to the left of this sarsen stone is one of the bluestones that are part of the Stonehenge mystery. *(Courtesy of the British Tourist Authority)*

The Great Serpent Mound in southeastern Ohio. The head of the serpent appears to be swallowing an egg-shaped object. This particular mound has no bodies or artifacts within, although many of the Mound Builders' other structures do. Other mounds were temple sites for the Mound Builders' religion. *(Courtesy of the Ohio Historical Society)*

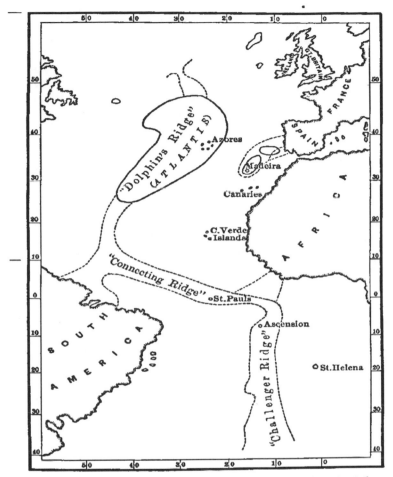

A map from Ignatius Donnelly's book *Atlantis: The Antediluvian World*. Donnelly was not content with "discovering" the location of the mythical continent of Atlantis. He tried to prove that it was the source of many of the world's civilizations, and drew ridges connecting it to both South America and Africa. *(Courtesy of the New York Public Library)*